초등 영어 구동사 160

하루 한 장의 기적

Giovanna Stapleton, Anne Kim 지음

동양북스

초등
영어
구동사
160

초판 1쇄 인쇄 | 2023년 3월 15일
초판 1쇄 발행 | 2023년 4월 1일

지은이 | Giovanna Stapleton, Anne Kim
발행인 | 김태웅
기획·총괄 | 황준
편집 | 안현진
디자인 | Design MOON-C
마케팅 | 나재승
제 작 | 현대순

발행처 | (주)동양북스
등   록 | 제 2014-000055호
주   소 | 서울시 마포구 동교로 22길 14 (04030)
구입 문의 | 전화 (02)337-1737
             팩스 (02)334-6624
내용 문의 | 전화 (02)337-1763
dybooks2@gmail.com

ISBN 979-11-5768-867-8 63740

머리말

구동사란 무엇일까요? 구동사는 동사가 전치사나 부사와 함께 쓰이는 표현이에요. 말이 어렵게 느껴질 수 있지만 아마 여러분은 실제로 구동사를 너무나 많이 사용하고 있을 겁니다. '일어나다' get up, '운동하다' work out처럼 늘 사용하는 것이기 때문이죠.

그런데 이처럼 늘 사용하는 동사 표현이지만 이 구동사는 막상 배울 때는 쉽지 않아요. 구동사가 되면서 새로운 뜻으로 변신을 하기 때문이죠. 예를 들어, see는 '보다', off는 '~로부터 떨어진'이라는 뜻이지만 see off가 함께 쓰이면 '~를 배웅하다'라는 뜻이 돼요. 이렇게 단어의 의미가 바뀌기 때문에 어떤 구동사는 의미를 쉽게 추측하기 어려워요.

하지만 그런데도 구동사가 많이 쓰이는 데는 이유가 있겠죠? 네, 맞아요. 구동사를 쓰면 다양한 상황을 훨씬 더 쉽고 간단하게 표현할 수 있어요. 예를 들어 see off를 알고 있다면 '그를 공항에서 배웅할 거예요.'를 다음과 같이 말할 거예요.

I will see him off at the airport.

하지만 만약 see off를 모른다면 어떻게 말해야 할까요?

I will go to the airport and say goodbye to him.

이렇게 말해도 뜻은 통하겠지만 문장이 길고 복잡해지지요? 그래서 원어민들은 구동사를 써서 훨씬 더 쉽게 표현하는 거예요. 실제로 구동사는 우리가 보는 영어 교과서, 리딩 교재, 원서 등에 정말 많이 쓰이고 있어요.

그럼 구동사는 어떤 것부터 익혀야 할까요? 이 책을 통해 초등 영어 교과서, 리딩 교재, 원서에 밥 먹듯이 나오는 구동사 160개부터 먼저 익혀보세요. 그러면 영어가 한층 더 쉽게 느껴질 거예요. 그럼 이제부터 100일간의 구동사 여행을 시작해볼까요?

Contents

이 책의 활용법

본문
본문

① 영어 교과서, 리딩 교재, 원서에서 가장 많이 쓰는 구동사를 배울 수 있어요. 하루에 구동사 2개씩만 꼭 익혀보세요.

② 구동사의 의미를 쉽게 이해할 수 있도록 그림과 함께 짧은 예문을 제시했어요.

③ 짧은 예문 → 긴 예문 → 대화문의 순서로 차근차근 배울 수 있도록 구성했어요. 다양한 예문과 함께 활용력을 높여보세요.

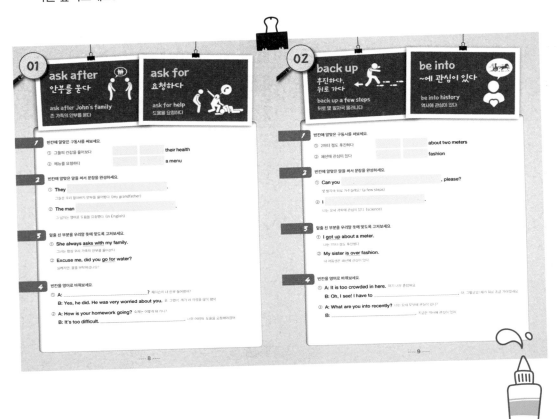

참고

✔ 구동사에서 부사가 쓰이는 경우에는 분리할 수 있어요.
I will see off John at the airport tomorrow.
I will see John off at the airport tomorrow.

✔ 이때 목적어가 대명사인 경우에는 반드시 부사 앞에 넣어야 해요.
I will see him off at the airport tomorrow.
~~I will see off him at the airport tomorrow.~~

Review

① 구동사를 익힐 때 복습은 필수예요. 자주 반복해주면 긴 시간을 들이지 않아도 구동사를 효율적으로 익힐 수 있어요.

② 절대 눈으로만 보면 안 돼요! 꼭 소리 내어 자연스럽게 의미가 떠오를 때까지 여러 번 읽고 써보세요.

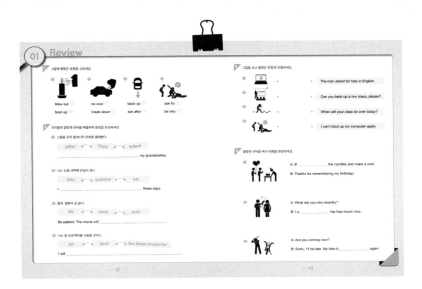

마인드맵 만들기

범주화(Categorization)를 해서 마인드맵을 만들어보세요. 중심에 동사/전치사/부사를 두고 구동사를 묶을 수 있을 거예요. 이렇게 범주화하면 기억할 때 도움이 돼요.

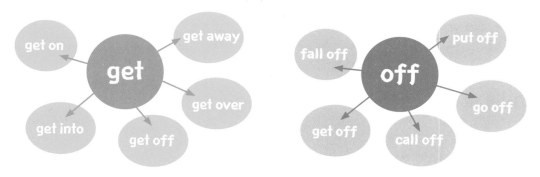

나만의 문장 만들기

예문을 다 익혔다면 나만의 문장을 만들어보세요. 주어나 부사(구)만 바꿔봐도 괜찮아요. 문장을 직접 만들 수 있으면 그 구동사는 내 것이 됩니다.

ask after
안부를 묻다

ask after John's family
존 가족의 안부를 묻다

ask for
요청하다

ask for help
도움을 요청하다

---

1 빈칸에 알맞은 구동사를 써보세요.

① 그들의 건강을 물어보다 _____ _____ their health

② 메뉴를 요청하다 _____ _____ a menu

---

2 빈칸에 알맞은 말을 써서 문장을 완성하세요.

① **They** _____ .

그들은 우리 할아버지 안부를 물어봤다. (my grandfather)

② **The man** _____ .

그 남자는 영어로 도움을 요청했다. (in English)

---

3 밑줄 친 부분을 우리말 뜻에 맞도록 고쳐보세요.

① **She always asks with my family.**

그녀는 항상 우리 가족의 안부를 물어본다.

② **Excuse me, did you go for water?**

실례지만, 물을 부탁하셨나요?

---

4 빈칸을 영어로 바꿔보세요.

① **A:** _____? 제이슨이 내 안부 물어봤어?

   B: Yes, he did. He was very worried about you. 응, 그랬어. 걔가 네 걱정을 많이 했어.

② **A: How is your homework going?** 숙제는 어떻게 돼 가니?

   B: It's too difficult. _____. 너무 어려워. 도움을 요청해야겠어.

back up
후진하다,
뒤로 가다

back up a few steps
뒤로 몇 발자국 물러나다

be into
~에 관심이 있다

be into history
역사에 관심이 있다

---

1 빈칸에 알맞은 구동사를 써보세요.

① 2미터 정도 후진하다 ☐☐☐☐ ☐☐☐☐ about two meters

② 패션에 관심이 있다 ☐☐☐☐ ☐☐☐☐ fashion

2 빈칸에 알맞은 말을 써서 문장을 완성하세요.

① **Can you** ☐☐☐☐☐☐☐☐☐☐☐ **, please?**

몇 발자국 뒤로 가주실래요? (a few steps)

② **I** ☐☐☐☐☐☐☐☐☐☐ **.**

나는 요새 과학에 관심이 있다. (science)

3 밑줄 친 부분을 우리말 뜻에 맞도록 고쳐보세요.

① **I <u>got up</u> about a meter.**

나는 1미터 정도 후진했다.

② **My sister <u>is over</u> fashion.**

내 여동생은 패션에 관심이 있다.

4 빈칸을 영어로 바꿔보세요.

① **A: It is too crowded in here.** 여기 너무 혼잡해요.

B: Oh, I see! I have to _____. 아, 그렇군요! 제가 뒤로 조금 가야겠네요.

② **A: What are you into recently?** 너는 요새 무엇에 관심이 있니?

B: _____. 지금은 역사에 관심이 있어.

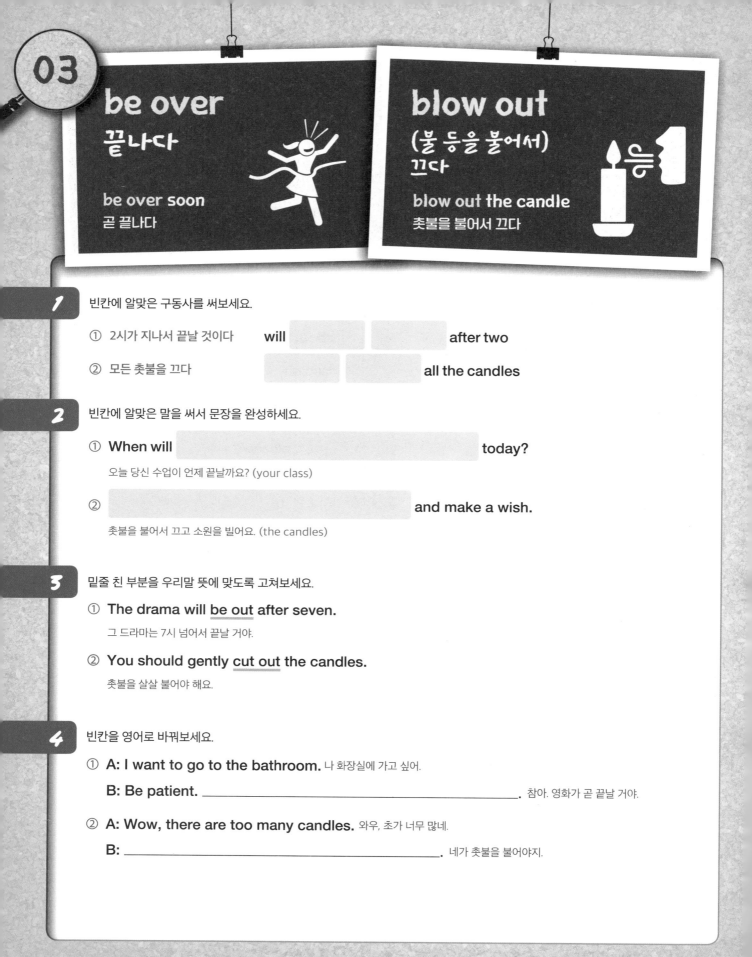

03

be over
끝나다

be over soon
곧 끝나다

blow out
(불 등을 불어서) 끄다

blow out the candle
촛불을 불어서 끄다

---

1 빈칸에 알맞은 구동사를 써보세요.

① 2시가 지나서 끝날 것이다   will _____ _____ after two

② 모든 촛불을 끄다   _____ _____ all the candles

2 빈칸에 알맞은 말을 써서 문장을 완성하세요.

① When will _____ today?

오늘 당신 수업이 언제 끝날까요? (your class)

② _____ and make a wish.

촛불을 불어서 끄고 소원을 빌어요. (the candles)

3 밑줄 친 부분을 우리말 뜻에 맞도록 고쳐보세요.

① The drama will <u>be out</u> after seven.

그 드라마는 7시 넘어서 끝날 거야.

② You should gently <u>cut out</u> the candles.

촛불을 살살 불어야 해요.

4 빈칸을 영어로 바꿔보세요.

① A: I want to go to the bathroom. 나 화장실에 가고 싶어.

B: Be patient. _____. 참아. 영화가 곧 끝날 거야.

② A: Wow, there are too many candles. 와우, 초가 너무 많네.

B: _____. 네가 촛불을 불어야지.

---- 10 ----

boot up
부팅하다, 작동시키다

boot up the computer
컴퓨터를 부팅하다

break down
고장 나다

suddenly break down
갑자기 고장 나다

1 빈칸에 알맞은 구동사를 써보세요.

① 노트북 컴퓨터를 부팅하다 [ ] [ ] the laptop

② 또 고장 나다 [ ] [ ] again

2 빈칸에 알맞은 말을 써서 문장을 완성하세요.

① **I can't** [   ].

나는 내 컴퓨터를 또 작동시킬 수가 없다. (my computer)

② **My bike** [   ].

내 자전거가 갑자기 고장 났다. (suddenly)

3 밑줄 친 부분을 우리말 뜻에 맞도록 고쳐보세요.

① **I will back up the beam projector.**

나는 빔 프로젝터를 작동시킬 거야.

② **His car suddenly took down on the road.**

그의 차가 갑자기 도로에서 고장 났다.

4 빈칸을 영어로 바꿔보세요.

① **A: What's the problem?** 무슨 일이야?

B: _____. 내 오래된 컴퓨터를 또 부팅할 수가 없어.

② **A: Are you coming now?** 너 지금 오고 있어?

B: Sorry, I'll be late. _____. 미안해, 늦을 것 같아. 내 자전거가 또 고장 났어.

1 그림에 알맞은 표현을 고르세요.

① blow out ☐
boot up ☐

② be over ☐
break down ☐

③ back up ☐
ask after ☐

④ ask for ☐
be into ☐

2 우리말에 알맞게 단어를 배열하여 문장을 완성하세요.

① 그들을 우리 할머니의 안부를 물어봤다.

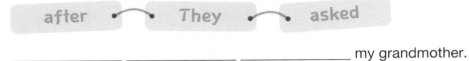

after • They • asked

_____ _____ _____ my grandmother.

② 나는 요즘 과학에 관심이 있다.

into • science • am

I _____ _____ _____ these days.

③ 참아. 영화가 곧 끝나.

be • soon • over

Be patient. The movie will _____ _____ _____.

④ 나는 빔 프로젝터를 시동할 것이다.

up • boot • the beam projector

I will _____ _____ _____.

3 그림을 보고 알맞은 문장과 연결하세요.

❶
         The man asked for help in English.

❷
         Can you back up a few steps, please?

❸
         When will your class be over today?

❹
         I can't boot up my computer again.

4 알맞은 단어를 써서 대화를 완성하세요.

❶

A: B_____ _____ the candles and make a wish.

B: Thanks for remembering my birthday!

❷

A: What are you into recently?

B: I a_____ _____ hip-hop music now.

❸

A: Are you coming now?

B: Sorry, I'll be late. My bike b_____ _____ again.

break into
침입하다 ▶

break into the house
집에 침입하다

break out
발생하다

A fire broke out.
불이 났다.

---

1 빈칸에 알맞은 구동사를 써보세요.

① 그의 사무실에 침입하다 [_____] [_____] **his office**

② 싸움이 일어났다. **A fight** [_____] [_____].

2 빈칸에 알맞은 말을 써서 문장을 완성하세요.

① **A thief** [_____].

　　도둑이 우리 집에 침입했다. (my house)

② **A big fire** [_____].

　　시내에서 큰불이 났다. (downtown)

3 밑줄 친 부분을 우리말 뜻에 맞도록 고쳐보세요.

① **A man with a mask is trying to break out the car.**

　　복면을 쓴 남자가 차에 침입하려고 하고 있다.

② **A fight carried out between two groups.**

　　두 집단 사이에서 싸움이 일어났다.

4 빈칸을 영어로 바꿔보세요.

① **A: What happened? You look worried.** 무슨 일이야? 걱정이 있어 보여.

　　B: _____. 지난밤에 우리 집에 도둑이 들었어.

② **A:** _____ **during the night.** 밤사이에 시내에 불이 났어.

　　B: Oh, really? I didn't know that. 아, 정말? 난 그건 몰랐어.

bring back
돌려주다

bring back the camera
카메라를 돌려주다

bring over
데려오다,
가져오다

bring him over
그를 데려오다

---

1 빈칸에 알맞은 구동사를 써보세요.

① 책을 돌려주다   ☐ ☐ the book

② 샌드위치를 가져오다   ☐ ☐ some sandwiches

---

2 빈칸에 알맞은 말을 써서 문장을 완성하세요.

① **When will you** _____ **?**

태블릿 언제 돌려줄 거야? (the tablet)

② **I will** _____.

내가 오늘 줄리안을 데려올 거야. (Julian)

---

3 밑줄 친 부분을 우리말 뜻에 맞도록 고쳐보세요.

① **I'll bring down your book by tomorrow.**

네 책을 내일까지 돌려줄게.

② **Jake is taking over his friend tonight.**

제이크가 오늘 밤 그의 친구를 데려올 거야.

---

4 빈칸을 영어로 바꿔보세요.

① **A: Can I borrow your tablet?** 네 태블릿을 빌릴 수 있을까?

   B: _____? 언제 그걸 돌려줄 거야?

② **A: Are you coming to the party?** 파티에 올 거야?

   B: Sure. And _____. 물론이지. 그리고 내가 오늘 밤 브래드도 데려갈게.

---

bring up
(말 등을) 꺼내다

bring up the topic
그 주제를 꺼내다

burst into
갑자기 ~하기 시작하다

burst into tears
울음을 터뜨리다

---

1 빈칸에 알맞은 구동사를 써보세요.

① 아이디어를 꺼내다 　　　　　　　　　 **the idea**

② 웃음을 터뜨리다 　　　　　　　　　 **laughter**

2 빈칸에 알맞은 말을 써서 문장을 완성하세요.

① **She** 　　　　　　　　　　　　　 .

　　그녀는 그 주제를 꺼냈다. (the topic)

② **Why did they** 　　　　　　　　　　　 ?

　　그들이 왜 갑자기 웃음을 터뜨렸어? (laughter)

3 밑줄 친 부분을 우리말 뜻에 맞도록 고쳐보세요.

① **I brought down the idea of a school trip.**

　　나는 수학 여행에 대한 아이디어를 꺼냈다.

② **My sister got into tears because of her test result.**

　　시험 결과 때문에 내 여동생은 울음을 터뜨렸다.

4 빈칸을 영어로 바꿔보세요.

① **A: Did you talk to Amy about David?** 에이미한테 데이비드에 대해 말했어?

　　B: _____ **with her. She gets very angry.**

　　그녀한테 그 주제는 꺼내지 마. 그녀가 아주 화를 내.

② **A:** _____ ? 그녀는 왜 갑자기 울음을 터뜨렸어?

　　B: She failed the exam. 그녀는 시험에 떨어졌어.

08

call back
다시 전화하다

call back several times
여러 번 다시 전화하다

call off
취소하다

call off the field trip
현장 학습을 취소하다

---

1 빈칸에 알맞은 구동사를 써보세요.

① 오늘 오후에 그에게 다시 전화할 것이다   will   ⬚   him   ⬚   this afternoon

② 경기를 취소하다   ⬚   ⬚   the game

2 빈칸에 알맞은 말을 써서 문장을 완성하세요.

① I ⬚ .

나는 여러 번 다시 전화했다. (several times)

② They ⬚ .

그들은 야구 경기를 취소했다. (the baseball game)

3 밑줄 친 부분을 우리말 뜻에 맞도록 고쳐보세요.

① I'll **bring him back** this afternoon.

오늘 오후에 그에게 다시 전화할 거야.

② My friend **got off** our trip at the last minute.

내 친구는 마지막 순간에 여행을 취소했다.

4 빈칸을 영어로 바꿔보세요.

① **A: Did you speak to Wayne yesterday?** 어제 웨인하고 이야기해 봤어?

B: No, but _____. 아니, 하지만 오늘 오후에 그에게 다시 전화할 거야.

② **A: It's going to rain a lot next week.** 다음 주에 비가 많이 올 거야.

B: _____ **then?** 그러면 우리 축구 경기를 취소하는 거야?

---

1 그림에 알맞은 표현을 고르세요.

❶ break into ☐
call back ☐

❷ bring back ☐
break out ☐

❸ burst into ☐
bring up ☐

❹ call off ☐
bring over ☐

2 우리말에 알맞게 단어를 배열하여 문장을 완성하세요.

❶ 두 집단 사이에서 싸움이 일어났다.

broke　A fight　out

_____ _____ _____ between two groups.

❷ 제이크가 오늘 밤 그의 친구를 데려올 거야.

over　is　bringing

Jake _____ _____ _____ his friend tonight.

❸ 오늘 오후에 그에게 다시 전화할 거야.

him　call　back

I'll _____ _____ _____ this afternoon.

❹ 그들은 경기를 취소했다.

called　the game　off

They _____ _____ _____.

3 그림을 보고 알맞은 문장과 연결하세요.

❶   •   • I called back several times.

❷   •   • He brought up the topic.

❸   •   • I will bring him over tonight.

❹   •   • A big fire broke out downtown.

4 알맞은 단어를 써서 대화를 완성하세요.

❶

A: Why did she b_____ _____ tears?

B: She failed the exam.

❷

A: Can I borrow your book?

B: When will you b_____ it _____?

❸

A: Can you talk now?

B: I'm sorry. I'll c_____ you _____ this afternoon.

09

call out
큰 소리로 외치다

call out to her sister
그녀의 언니에게 큰 소리로 외치다

call up
전화하다

call them up
그들에게 전화하다

---

1 빈칸에 알맞은 구동사를 써보세요.

① 아주 큰 소리로 그에게 외치다   very loudly to him

② 그녀에게 전화하다   her

2 빈칸에 알맞은 말을 써서 문장을 완성하세요.

① **Jamie**   .

제이미는 도와 달라고 엄마한테 큰 소리로 외쳤다. (for help)

② **I'll**   .

나는 이번 주에 그들에게 전화할 것이다. (this week)

3 밑줄 친 부분을 우리말 뜻에 맞도록 고쳐보세요.

① **I <u>called back</u> loudly to him.**

나는 그에게 아주 큰 소리로 말했다.

② **I'll <u>call her off</u> after class.**

나는 수업 후에 그녀에게 전화할 것이다.

4 빈칸을 영어로 바꿔보세요.

① **A:** _____? 도와 달라고 큰 소리로 외쳤어?

B: Yes, a teacher helped me. 응, 선생님 한 분이 도와주셨어.

② **A: Did you invite everyone to the party?** 너 파티에 모두 초대했어?

B: No, but _____. 아니, 하지만 이번 주말에 그들에게 전화할 거야.

10

care about
신경 쓰다
care about
your health
당신의 건강을 신경 쓰다

care for
보살피다
care for a sick cat
아픈 고양이를 보살피다

1 빈칸에 알맞은 구동사를 써보세요.

① 타인의 감정을 신경 쓰다 ☐ ☐ other people's feelings

② 나이 든 환자들을 보살피다 ☐ ☐ elderly patients

2 빈칸에 알맞은 말을 써서 문장을 완성하세요.

① I really ☐ .

난 너를 정말 많이 신경 쓰고 있어. (a lot)

② Vets ☐ .

수의사들은 아픈 애완동물들을 보살핀다. (pets)

3 밑줄 친 부분을 우리말 뜻에 맞도록 고쳐보세요.

① She doesn't <u>worry about</u> other people's feelings.

그녀는 다른 사람의 감정을 신경 쓰지 않는다.

② Who is <u>looking for</u> your son while you are at work?

당신이 회사에 있을 때 누가 당신 아들을 보살피나요?

4 빈칸을 영어로 바꿔보세요.

① A: Isn't she really selfish? 그녀는 정말 이기적이지 않아?

B: Yeah. _____ but herself.

응. 그녀는 자기 자신 이외에는 다른 사람은 신경 쓰지 않아.

② A: _____? 누가 환자들을 돌보게 되나요?

B: Our medical team will do that. 우리 의료팀이 보살필 거예요.

calm down
진정하다

Please calm down.
진정해요.

carry out
수행하다

carry out a task
과제를 수행하다

1 빈칸에 알맞은 구동사를 써보세요.

① 잠깐 진정하다   ☐☐☐☐   for a second

② 설문을 수행하다   ☐☐☐☐   a survey

2 빈칸에 알맞은 말을 써서 문장을 완성하세요.

① ☐☐☐☐☐☐ and breathe!

조금 진정하고 숨을 쉬어 봐! (a bit)

② **We have to** ☐☐☐☐☐☐ .

우리는 임무를 수행해야 한다. (the mission)

3 밑줄 친 부분을 우리말 뜻에 맞도록 고쳐보세요.

① **We're not in a rush. <u>Hand down</u> and take your time.**

서두르지 않아도 돼. 진정하고 천천히 해.

② **We should <u>point out</u> a survey for the report.**

우리는 보고서를 위해 설문을 수행해야 해요.

4 빈칸을 영어로 바꿔보세요.

① **A: I think** _____. 너 진정해야 할 것 같아.

B: But we don't have enough time. 하지만 우리 시간이 충분하지 않아.

② **A: What am I supposed to do?** 내가 어떻게 해야 하죠?

B: You should _____. 지금 당장 그 계획을 실행해야 해요.

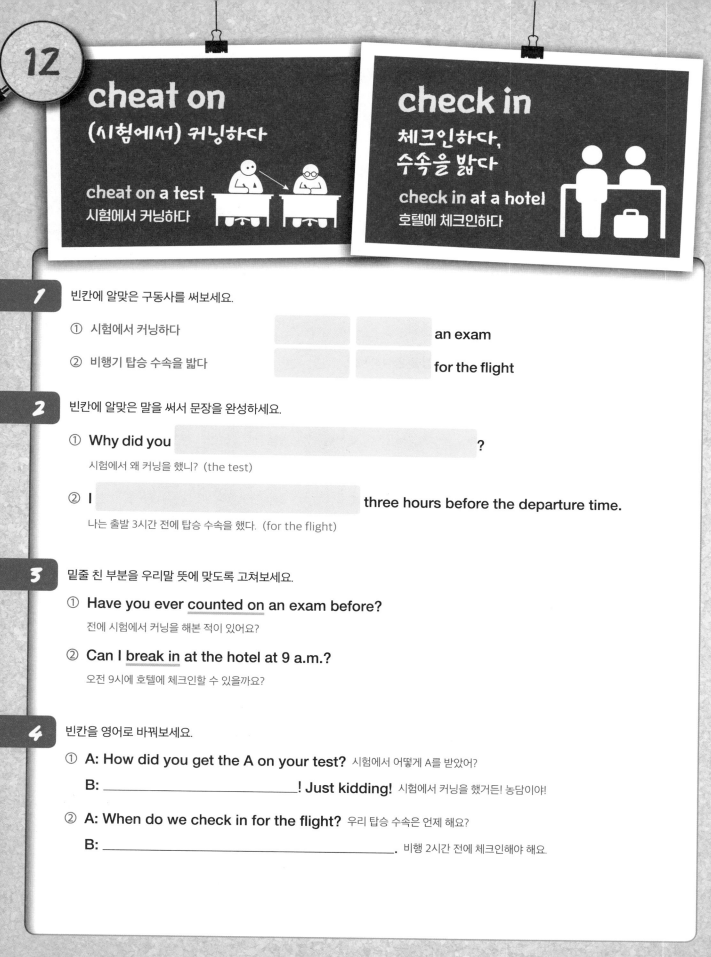

12

cheat on
(시험에서) 커닝하다

cheat on a test
시험에서 커닝하다

check in
체크인하다, 수속을 밟다

check in at a hotel
호텔에 체크인하다

---

1 빈칸에 알맞은 구동사를 써보세요.

① 시험에서 커닝하다   _____ _____ **an exam**

② 비행기 탑승 수속을 밟다   _____ _____ **for the flight**

2 빈칸에 알맞은 말을 써서 문장을 완성하세요.

① **Why did you _____ ?**

시험에서 왜 커닝을 했니? (the test)

② **I _____ three hours before the departure time.**

나는 출발 3시간 전에 탑승 수속을 했다. (for the flight)

3 밑줄 친 부분을 우리말 뜻에 맞도록 고쳐보세요.

① **Have you ever <u>counted on</u> an exam before?**

전에 시험에서 커닝을 해본 적이 있어요?

② **Can I <u>break in</u> at the hotel at 9 a.m.?**

오전 9시에 호텔에 체크인할 수 있을까요?

4 빈칸을 영어로 바꿔보세요.

① **A: How did you get the A on your test?** 시험에서 어떻게 A를 받았어?

     B: _____! Just kidding! 시험에서 커닝을 했거든! 농담이야!

② **A: When do we check in for the flight?** 우리 탑승 수속은 언제 해요?

     B: _____. 비행 2시간 전에 체크인해야 해요.

1 그림에 알맞은 표현을 고르세요.

❶

❷

❸

❹

call out ☐

care about ☐

call up ☐

check in ☐

carry out ☐

care for ☐

cheat on ☐

calm down ☐

2 우리말에 알맞게 단어를 배열하여 문장을 완성하세요.

❶ 난 내일 그에게 전화할 것이다.

I'll ＿＿＿＿＿＿ ＿＿＿＿＿＿ ＿＿＿＿＿＿ tomorrow.

❷ 수의사들은 아픈 애완동물들을 보살핀다.

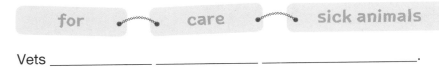

Vets ＿＿＿＿＿＿ ＿＿＿＿＿＿ ＿＿＿＿＿＿.

❸ 우리는 임무를 수행해야 한다.

We have to ＿＿＿＿＿＿ ＿＿＿＿＿＿ ＿＿＿＿＿＿.

❹ 전에 시험에서 커닝을 해본 적이 있어요?

Have you ever ＿＿＿＿＿＿ ＿＿＿＿＿＿ ＿＿＿＿＿＿ before?

3 그림을 보고 알맞은 문장과 연결하세요.

❶   •

• You should care about your health.

❷   •

• I called out very loudly to my sister.

❸   •

• Calm down a bit and breathe!

❹   •

• Can I check in at the hotel at 9 a.m.?

4 알맞은 단어를 써서 대화를 완성하세요.

❶

A: Did you c_____ him _____ yesterday?

B: No, I was very busy. I'll call him up now.

❷

A: Who c_____ _____ the sick animals?

B: Our vets did that.

❸

A: When do we c_____ _____ for the flight?

B: We should check in two hours before the flight.

13

cheer up
격려하다

Cheer up, everyone!
모두 힘냅시다!

chill out
긴장을 풀다

chill out in front of the TV
TV를 보며 긴장을 풀다

1 빈칸에 알맞은 구동사를 써보세요.

① 실망한 사람들을 격려하다   the disappointed people

② 앉아서 긴장을 풀어!   Sit down and   !

2 빈칸에 알맞은 말을 써서 문장을 완성하세요.

①   .

힘내고 그 일은 잊어버려. (forget)

② **You look so tense.**   !

너 너무 긴장한 것처럼 보여. 좀 긴장 풀어! (just)

3 밑줄 친 부분을 우리말 뜻에 맞도록 고쳐보세요.

① <u>Back up</u>! Things aren't really that bad.

힘내! 상황이 그렇게 안 좋은 건 아니야.

② <u>Carry out</u> and think about this, okay?

긴장을 풀고 이것을 생각해봐, 알았지?

4 빈칸을 영어로 바꿔보세요.

① A: **We're going to lose the game.** 우리가 경기에 질 거 같아.

    B: _____! The game is not over yet.

       모두 힘내자! 경기는 아직 끝나지 않았어.

② A: **It was a long day.** _____ in front of the TV.

       긴 하루였어. TV를 보면서 긴장을 풀어야겠어.

    B: **That's a great idea. I'll join you.** 좋은 생각이야. 나도 같이 볼래.

catch up with

~를 따라잡다
catch up with him
그를 따라잡다

come across

우연히 만나다, 우연히 발견하다

come across
the classmate
반 친구를 우연히 만나다

1 빈칸에 알맞은 구동사를 써보세요.

① 선두주자를 따라잡다 _____ _____ _____ the front-runner

② 흥미로운 이야기를 발견하다 _____ _____ an interesting story

2 빈칸에 알맞은 말을 써서 문장을 완성하세요.

① I can't _____.

나는 그를 따라잡을 수 없다. (him)

② I _____ in town.

나는 동네에서 예전 학교 친구를 우연히 만났다. (an old school friend)

3 밑줄 친 부분을 우리말 뜻에 맞도록 고쳐보세요.

① Please go ahead. I'll <u>come up with</u> you later.

먼저 가세요. 전 나중에 뒤따라갈게요.

② I <u>came out</u> this book at the library.

나는 도서관에서 이 책을 우연히 발견했다.

4 빈칸을 영어로 바꿔보세요.

① A: Your mom has just left. 너희 엄마 방금 출발하셨어.

B: _____ if I run fast. 내가 빨리 뛰어가면 엄마를 따라잡을 수 있어.

② A: _____? 전에 그들을 우연히 만난 적이 있어요?

B: No, I haven't. 아뇨, 없어요.

come out
나오다

A new album will come out.
새 앨범이 나올 예정이다.

come over
멀리서 오다,
들르다

come over for supper
저녁 먹으러 들르다

---

1 빈칸에 알맞은 구동사를 써보세요.

① 마침내 나오다 ⬜⬜ ⬜⬜ **at last**

② 우리 집에 들르다 ⬜⬜ ⬜⬜ **to my place**

---

2 빈칸에 알맞은 말을 써서 문장을 완성하세요.

① **The animals only** ⬜⬜⬜⬜⬜⬜⬜ .

그 동물들은 밤에만 나온다. (at night)

② **Many foreigners** ⬜⬜⬜⬜⬜⬜ **during the Olympics.**

올림픽 동안 많은 외국인들이 서울에 들렀다. (Seoul)

---

3 밑줄 친 부분을 우리말 뜻에 맞도록 고쳐보세요.

① **The sun blew out at last.**

마침내 해가 나왔다.

② **Emma sometimes gets over to my house.**

엠마는 가끔 우리 집에 들른다.

---

4 빈칸을 영어로 바꿔보세요.

① **A: Your favorite boy band's new album is** _____ .

네가 좋아하는 남자 그룹의 새 앨범이 곧 나올 거야.

B: I know. I am waiting for it. 알아. 나도 그걸 기다리고 있어.

② **A: Did you enjoy your dinner?** 저녁 식사 맛있게 드셨나요?

B: Yes, it was lovely. _____ .

네, 너무 좋았어요. 조만간 저희 또 들를게요.

---

come up with
생각해 내다
come up with an answer
답을 생각해 내다

consist of
구성되다
consist of three parts
3부로 구성되다

1 빈칸에 알맞은 구동사를 써보세요.

① 해결책을 생각해 내다   [　　　] [　　　] [　　　] a solution

② 밥과 감자로 구성되다   [　　　] [　　　] rice and potatoes

2 빈칸에 알맞은 말을 써서 문장을 완성하세요.

① **Never expect him to** [　　　　　　　　　　].

그가 멋진 아이디어를 생각해 낼 거라는 기대는 절대 하지 마. (a brilliant idea)

② **Our basketball team** [　　　　　　　　　].

우리 농구팀은 9명의 선수로 구성되어 있다. (nine players)

3 밑줄 친 부분을 우리말 뜻에 맞도록 고쳐보세요.

① **He caught up with a solution to our problem.**

그는 우리 문제에 대한 해결책을 생각해 냈다.

② **This dish comes mainly of rice and potatoes.**

이 요리는 주로 밥과 감자로 구성돼 있다.

4 빈칸을 영어로 바꿔보세요.

① **A: I'm in big trouble.** 나 큰 곤경에 처했어.

B: Let's ask John. He can _____.

존한테 물어보자. 그는 항상 해결책을 생각해 내잖아.

② **A: Do we get a free lunch?** 점심을 무료로 먹는 거야?

B: Yes, you will. _____. 응, 그럴 거야. 샌드위치와 과일로 구성돼 있어.

1 그림에 알맞은 표현을 고르세요.

❶

cheer up ▢

come across ▢

❷

chill out ▢

catch up with ▢

❸

come over ▢

come out ▢

❹

come up with ▢

consist of ▢

2 우리말에 알맞게 단어를 배열하여 문장을 완성하세요.

❶ 힘내고 그 일은 잊어버려.

Cheer • and • up

_____ _____ _____ forget about it.

❷ 나는 그를 따라잡을 수 없다.

with • catch • up

I can't _____ _____ _____ him.

❸ 그 동물들은 밤에만 나온다.

at night • come • out

The animals only _____ _____ _____ .

❹ 그는 우리 문제에 대한 해결책을 생각해 냈다.

with • up • came

He _____ _____ _____ a solution to our problem.

3 그림을 보고 알맞은 문장과 연결하세요.

❶ • • Cheer up, everyone!

❷ • • I came across an old school friend in town.

❸ • • This book consists of three parts.

❹ • • She sometimes comes over to my house.

4 알맞은 단어를 써서 대화를 완성하세요.

❶

A: I'm so tired. I need to c_____ _____ in front of the TV.

B: That's a great idea. I'll join you.

❷

A: Your mom has just left.

B: I can c_____ _____ _____ her if I run fast.

❸

A: My favorite singer's new album is c_____ _____ soon.

B: Wow! You are really looking forward to it.

count on
믿다, 기대하다

count on him
그를 믿다

cover up
숨기다

cover up the truth
진실을 감추다

---

1 빈칸에 알맞은 구동사를 써보세요.

① 우리를 믿다　　　　　　　　　　　　　　　　　us

② 실수를 감추다　　　　　　　　　　　　　　　　the mistakes

2 빈칸에 알맞은 말을 써서 문장을 완성하세요.

① **You can** _____ .

　　너는 지금부터 우리를 믿어도 돼. (from now on)

② **She tried to** _____ .

　　그녀는 범죄를 숨기려고 했다. (the crime)

3 밑줄 친 부분을 우리말 뜻에 맞도록 고쳐보세요.

① **Can I <u>get on</u> your loyalty?**

　　네 의리를 믿어도 될까?

② **You can't <u>call up</u> the truth forever.**

　　넌 진실을 영원히 감출 수는 없어.

4 빈칸을 영어로 바꿔보세요.

① **A:** _____? 내가 그녀는 믿을 수 있을까?

　　B: Sure. She will certainly help you. 물론이야. 그녀는 분명히 너를 도와줄 거야.

② **A:** _____ **for your friend?**

　　너 네 친구를 위해 진실을 감추려고 하는 거야?

　　B: No, I'm telling you the truth! 아니야, 난 너한테 사실을 말하고 있는 거야!

18

cut down on
줄이다

cut down on sweets
단것을 줄이다

cut out
(모터, 엔진 등이)
갑자기 멎다, 서다

One of the engines cut out.
엔진 중 하나가 갑자기 멈췄다.

---

1 빈칸에 알맞은 구동사를 써보세요.

① 정크 푸드를 줄이다   junk food

② 인터넷이 갑자기 멎었다.   **The Internet suddenly**   .

2 빈칸에 알맞은 말을 써서 문장을 완성하세요.

① **I'm trying to**   .

나는 청량음료를 줄이려고 노력하고 있다. (soft drinks)

② **Oh my God,**   .

맙소사, 비행기 엔진이 갑자기 멎었어요. (the plane's engines)

3 밑줄 친 부분을 우리말 뜻에 맞도록 고쳐보세요.

① **We will <u>calm down on</u> expenses this year.**

우리는 올해 지출을 줄일 거예요.

② **Let me check the connection. The Wi-Fi has <u>put out</u> again.**

내가 접속을 살펴볼게. 와이파이가 또 갑자기 끊어졌어.

4 빈칸을 영어로 바꿔보세요.

① **A: I've gained a lot of weight.** 나 몸무게가 많이 늘었어.

     B: _____! 너 케이크를 줄여야 해!

② **A:** _____. 라디오가 갑자기 끊겼어요.

     B: Please wait until I fix it. 고칠 때까지 기다려 주세요.

do without
~없이 지내다

do without
sleep for a while
한동안 잠을 자지 않고 지내다

dress up
옷을 차려입다

dress up for the party
파티를 위해 옷을 차려입다

1 빈칸에 알맞은 구동사를 써보세요.

① 스마트폰 없이 지내다 　　　　　　 a smartphone

② 해적처럼 차려입다 　　　　　　 like a pirate

2 빈칸에 알맞은 말을 써서 문장을 완성하세요.

① **I can't** 　　　　　　 **!**

나는 네 조언 없이 할 수 없어! (advice)

② **She** 　　　　　　 **.**

그녀는 공주처럼 차려입었다. (as a princess)

3 밑줄 친 부분을 우리말 뜻에 맞도록 고쳐보세요.

① **In her work, she cannot do with a computer.**

자기 일을 할 때 그녀는 컴퓨터 없이 할 수 없다.

② **You don't need to make up to go to the mall.**

쇼핑몰 가려고 차려입을 필요는 없어.

4 빈칸을 영어로 바꿔보세요.

① **A: The French fries look yummy. Pass me the ketchup.** 감자 튀김이 맛있어 보여. 케첩 좀 건네줘.

B: We ran out. We'll have to _____ it today. 다 떨어졌어. 오늘은 케첩 없이 지내야 될 거야.

② **A: The dinner is a formal one.** 저녁 식사는 공식적인 자리야.

B: I'll go and _____ then. 그럼 나도 가서 차려입을게.

drop by
잠깐 들르다

drop by **a friend's house**
친구 집에 잠깐 들르다

eat out
외식하다

eat out **tonight**
오늘 밤에 외식하다

1 빈칸에 알맞은 구동사를 써보세요.

① 가게에 잠깐 들르다   the shop

② 매주 토요일에 외식하다   every Saturday

2 빈칸에 알맞은 말을 써서 문장을 완성하세요.

① **I just**   **home.**

나는 집에 가는 길에 그냥 들렀다. (on my way)

②   **today.**

우리 오늘 외식해요. (Let's)

3 밑줄 친 부분을 우리말 뜻에 맞도록 고쳐보세요.

① **Why don't we pass by a bakery on the way home?**

집에 가는 길에 빵 가게에 잠깐 들르는 거 어때?

② **We like to eat up on the weekends.**

우리는 주말엔 외식하는 것을 좋아해.

4 빈칸을 영어로 바꿔보세요.

① **A: Can you** _____ **and get some milk?**

가게 잠깐 들러서 우유 좀 사다 줄 수 있어?

B: Sure. I'll pick up some milk on my way home. 그럼. 집에 가는 길에 우유를 좀 사 갈게.

② **A: What do you want to eat for dinner?** 저녁에 뭐 먹고 싶어?

B: _____. 우리 오늘 밤에 외식하자.

1 그림에 알맞은 표현을 고르세요.

❶

cover up ☐

do without ☐

❷

cut down on ☐

count on ☐

❸

drop by ☐

dress up ☐

❹

cut out ☐

eat out ☐

2 우리말에 알맞게 단어를 배열하여 문장을 완성하세요.

❶ 너는 지금부터 우리한테 기대도 돼.

count ⌇ us ⌇ on

You can _____ _____ _____ from now on.

❷ 비행기 엔진이 갑자기 멎었어요.

out ⌇ have ⌇ cut

The plane's engines _____ _____ _____.

❸ 자기 일을 할 때 그녀는 컴퓨터 없이 할 수 없다.

a computer ⌇ without ⌇ do

In her work, she cannot _____ _____ _____.

❹ 집에 가는 길에 그냥 들렀어.

by ⌇ on my way ⌇ dropped

I just _____ _____ _____ home.

3 그림을 보고 알맞은 문장과 연결하세요.

❶   •   •   She tried to cover up the truth.

❷   •   •   Let's eat out today.

❸   •   •   I'm trying to cut down on sweets.

❹   •   •   She dressed up as a princess.

4 알맞은 단어를 써서 대화를 완성하세요.

❶
A: Please pass me the ketchup.

B: Sorry. We ran out. We'll have to d_____ _____ it today.

❷
A: You've gained a lot of weight.

B: I know. I'm trying to c_____ _____ on cake!

❸
A: Can you d_____ _____ the shop and get some milk?

B: Sure. I'll pick it up on my way home.

21

fall apart
부서지다,
산산조각이 나다

fall apart completely
완전히 부서지다

fall behind
뒤떨어지다, ~에 뒤지다

**fall behind with
her schoolwork**
학교 공부에 뒤처지다

---

1 빈칸에 알맞은 구동사를 써보세요.

① 내 나무집이 완전히 부서졌다.　　My tree house _____ _____ completely.

② 일정에 뒤처지다　　_____ _____ schedule

2 빈칸에 알맞은 말을 써서 문장을 완성하세요.

① _____ completely.

　모래성이 완전히 부서졌다. (the sandcastle)

② She _____ because she missed classes.

　그녀는 수업에 빠졌기 때문에 학교 공부에 뒤처졌다. (schoolwork)

3 밑줄 친 부분을 우리말 뜻에 맞도록 고쳐보세요.

① Mom bought me new shoes because my old ones <u>fell down</u>.

　내 오래된 신발이 다 떨어져서 엄마가 나에게 새 신발을 사주셨다.

② She really doesn't like to <u>leave behind</u> her rival.

　그녀는 그녀의 라이벌한테 뒤지는 것을 정말로 좋아하지 않는다.

4 빈칸을 영어로 바꿔보세요.

① A: I need a new bag. It's old now. 나는 새 가방이 필요해. 이제 그것은 낡았어.

　B: Yeah, it looks like _____. 그래, 다 망가져 가는 것처럼 보여.

② A: Wow, are you still practicing? 우와, 아직도 연습하고 있는 거야?

　B: Yes, _____. 응, 뒤처지고 싶지 않아.

22

fall off
떨어지다

fall off a ladder
사다리에서 떨어지다

feel down
기분이 우울하다

feel down because
of the rain
비 때문에 기분이 우울하다

---

1 빈칸에 알맞은 구동사를 써보세요.

① 침대에서 자주 떨어지다   often ☐ ☐ the bed

② 날씨 때문에 기분이 우울하다   ☐ ☐ because of the weather

2 빈칸에 알맞은 말을 써서 문장을 완성하세요.

① **Please be careful not to** ☐ .

말에서 떨어지지 않도록 조심하세요. (the horse)

② **I listen to music** ☐ .

나는 기분이 우울할 때 음악을 듣는다. (when)

3 밑줄 친 부분을 우리말 뜻에 맞도록 고쳐보세요.

① **She nearly <u>fell behind</u> the stage while she was dancing.**

그녀는 춤을 추다가 무대에서 거의 떨어질 뻔했다.

② **What do you do when you <u>break down</u>?**

너는 우울할 때 무엇을 하니?

4 빈칸을 영어로 바꿔보세요.

① **A: How did he get hurt?** 그는 어떻게 다쳤어?

    B: _____ **while he was riding.** 그는 자전거를 타다가 떨어졌어.

② **A: What's the matter with you?** 너 무슨 일 있어?

    B: It is okay. _____. 괜찮아. 오늘 그냥 기분이 우울하네.

---

figure out
(노력을 통해서) 알아내다

figure out the answer
답을 알아내다

fill out
작성하다

fill out this form
이 서류를 작성하다

---

1 빈칸에 알맞은 구동사를 써보세요.

① 진실을 알아내다   ⬜ ⬜ the truth

② 설문지를 작성하다   ⬜ ⬜ the survey

2 빈칸에 알맞은 말을 써서 문장을 완성하세요.

① **How did you** _____ ?

너는 그 단어의 뜻을 어떻게 알아냈어? (meaning)

② **Please** _____ .

아래의 양식을 작성해주세요. (below)

3 밑줄 친 부분을 우리말 뜻에 맞도록 고쳐보세요.

① **I can't come out the reason behind the error.**

나는 실수의 원인을 알아낼 수 없다.

② **Please figure out the landing card now.**

이제 입국 양식을 작성해주세요.

4 빈칸을 영어로 바꿔보세요.

① **A: Do you know the answer?** 너 정답을 아니?

B: I have no idea. _____. 전혀 모르겠어. 그것을 알아낼 수가 없어.

② **A: Pass out the handouts to everyone.** 모두에게 유인물을 전달해주세요.

B: Do we need to _____ **on the sheets?**

종이에 있는 모든 것을 작성해야 하나요?

find out
~에 대한 정보를 알아내다, 알게 되다
find out the difference
차이를 알게되다

get along with
~와 사이좋게 지내다
get along with everyone
모든 사람들과 잘 지내다

---

1 빈칸에 알맞은 구동사를 써보세요.

① 비밀번호를 알게 되다   ▢▢▢ ▢▢▢ the passwords

② 학급 친구들과 잘 지내다   ▢▢▢ ▢▢▢ ▢▢▢ classmates

2 빈칸에 알맞은 말을 써서 문장을 완성하세요.

① **You will** _____.

너는 곧 진실을 알게 될 것이다. (the truth)

② **Luckily, my dog** _____.

운이 좋게도, 우리 개는 고양이들하고 잘 지냈다. (the cats)

3 밑줄 친 부분을 우리말 뜻에 맞도록 고쳐보세요.

① **We filled out the results of the class elections.**

우리는 학급 선거 결과를 알게 됐다.

② **I get out of my siblings. I love them.**

나는 형제자매들하고 잘 지낸다. 나는 그들을 사랑한다.

4 빈칸을 영어로 바꿔보세요.

① **A:** _____. 마침내 그의 이메일 주소를 알게 됐어.

   B: Please text it to me. 나한테 문자로 보내주라.

② **A: My two kids don't seem to** _____.

   우리 집 두 아이는 서로 잘 지내는 것 같지 않아.

   B: Have you tried counseling? 상담을 시도해봤어?

1 그림에 알맞은 표현을 고르세요.

❶

fall apart ☐

fall off ☐

❷

find out ☐

fill out ☐

❸

fall behind ☐

feel down ☐

❹

figure out ☐

get along with ☐

2 우리말에 알맞게 단어를 배열하여 문장을 완성하세요.

❶ 그녀는 학교 수업에 뒤처졌다.

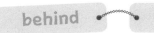

behind — with — fell

She _____ _____ _____ her schoolwork.

❷ 말에서 떨어지지 않도록 조심하세요.

off — the horse — fall

Please be careful not to _____ _____ _____.

❸ 나는 실수의 원인을 알아낼 수 없다.

out — figure — the reason

I cannot _____ _____ _____ behind the error.

❹ 나는 실제 이름과 주소를 알아냈어요.

out — have — found

I _____ _____ _____ the real name and address.

3 그림을 보고 알맞은 문장과 연결하세요.

❶   •   • I get along with everyone.

❷   •   • Please fill out the landing card now.

❸   •   • I feel down because of the rain.

❹   •   • The sandcastle fell apart completely!

4 알맞은 단어를 써서 대화를 완성하세요.

❶

A: I need new shoes. They are old now.

B: Yeah, it looks like they're f_____ _____.

❷

A: How did she get hurt?

B: She f_____ _____ her bicycle while she was riding.

❸

A: Do you know the answer?

B: I have no idea. I can't f_____ _____ _____.

get around
돌아다니다

get around by bike
자전거로 돌아다니다

get away
떠나다

get away from the crowds
무리에서 떠나다

---

1 빈칸에 알맞은 구동사를 써보세요.

① 소문이 파다하다.　　　　　　　　Word _____ _____ .

② 불타는 승용차에서 빠져나가다　　　_____ _____ from the burning car

2 빈칸에 알맞은 말을 써서 문장을 완성하세요.

① **She doesn't** _____ .

그녀는 요새 많이 돌아다니지 않는다. (much)

② **I'm going to** _____ .

나는 일주일 동안 떠나 있을 것이다. (for a week)

3 밑줄 친 부분을 우리말 뜻에 맞도록 고쳐보세요.

① **Walking is a cheap way to <u>turn around</u>.**

걷기는 싸게 돌아다닐 수 있는 방법이다.

② **We should <u>get off</u> somewhere nice!**

우리는 좋은 곳으로 떠나야만 해!

4 빈칸을 영어로 바꿔보세요.

① **A: How was your trip?** 여행은 어땠어?

　B: Good! It was so easy to _____ .

좋았어! 지하철로 돌아다니기 정말 쉬웠어.

② **A: What plans do you have after the test?** 시험 끝나고 무슨 계획 있어?

　B: I'm going to _____ . 가족들과 일주일 동안 떠날 거야.

get back
돌아오다

get back home
집에 돌아오다

get into
흥미를 갖게 되다

get into Latin music
라틴 음악에 흥미를 갖게 되다

1 빈칸에 알맞은 구동사를 써보세요.

① 주제로 돌아오다   to the topic

② 요즘 힙합에 흥미를 갖게 되다   hip-hop these days

2 빈칸에 알맞은 말을 써서 문장을 완성하세요.

① **When did she** ?

그녀는 여행에서 언제 돌아왔어? (her trip)

② **My dad and I have really** .

우리 아빠와 나는 보드게임에 정말 흥미를 가지게 되었다. (play boardgames)

3 밑줄 친 부분을 우리말 뜻에 맞도록 고쳐보세요.

① **What time will you take back?**

너는 몇 시에 돌아올 거야?

② **I have gotten around cake decorating.**

나는 케이크를 장식하는 것에 흥미를 갖게 되었다.

4 빈칸을 영어로 바꿔보세요.

① **A: When can we talk about it?** 그것에 대해 우리 언제 얘기할 수 있어?

B: I'll call you when _____. 오늘 오후에 돌아오면 내가 너한테 전화할게.

② **A: You are really** _____, **aren't you?**

너 진짜 축구에 흥미를 갖게 됐지, 그렇지 않니?

B: Yes, I watch EPL games every night. 맞아, 나는 매일 밤 프리미어 리그*를 봐. (*잉글랜드 프로축구 1부)

get off
내리다

get off a bus
버스에서 내리다

get on
타다

get on
the subway
지하철에 타다

1 빈칸에 알맞은 구동사를 써보세요.

① 여기서 내리다   [ ] [ ] here

② 기차에 타다   [ ] [ ] the train

2 빈칸에 알맞은 말을 써서 문장을 완성하세요.

① **We are** [ ].

우리는 다음 역에서 내릴 거예요. (the next station)

② [ ] **this morning.**

나는 오늘 아침에 버스를 잘못 탔다. (the wrong bus)

3 밑줄 친 부분을 우리말 뜻에 맞도록 고쳐보세요.

① **Which station should I <u>get on</u> at?**

저는 어떤 역에서 내려야 해요?

② **Watch your step when you <u>put on</u> the subway.**

지하철을 탈 때 발을 조심하세요.

4 빈칸을 영어로 바꿔보세요.

① **A:** _____**?** 그녀는 어디에서 버스에서 내렸어?

B: She got off at the terminal. 그녀는 터미널에서 내렸어.

② **A:** _____ **if you can't walk?**

걸을 수 없으면 어떻게 비행기에 탑승하나요?

B: We will help you with an aisle chair. 기내용 휠체어로 도와드릴 거예요.

get out of
~에서 내리다, 나가다

get out of here
여기서 나가다

get over
극복하다,
(병 등에서) 회복하다

get over the flu
독감에서 회복하다

---

1 빈칸에 알맞은 구동사를 써보세요.

① 길을 비키다 　　　　　　　　　　　　　　　**my way**

② 나쁜 경험을 극복하다 　　　　　　　　**a bad experience**

2 빈칸에 알맞은 말을 써서 문장을 완성하세요.

① **You have to** 　　　　　　　　　　　　.

지금 홍수 지역에서 벗어나야 해요. (the flood zone)

② **He** 　　　　　　　　　　　　　　.

그는 수줍음을 극복할 수 없다. (his shyness)

3 밑줄 친 부분을 우리말 뜻에 맞도록 고쳐보세요.

① **Get along with the building! It is falling apart!**

건물에서 나가세요! 건물이 무너지고 있어요!

② **It took her ages to go over the trauma.**

그녀는 트라우마를 극복하는 데 오래 걸렸어요.

4 빈칸을 영어로 바꿔보세요.

① **A: Do you want to live in a big city?** 너는 대도시에서 살고 싶어?

B: Yes, ＿＿＿＿＿＿＿＿＿＿＿＿＿＿＿＿＿**.** 응, 나는 이 작은 마을에서 벗어나고 싶어.

② **A: It is hard to** ＿＿＿＿＿＿＿＿＿＿＿＿＿＿**.**

내 개의 죽음을 극복하는 게 어려워.

B: I had the same experience last year. It is tough. 나도 작년에 같은 경험을 했어. 그것은 힘들어.

1 그림에 알맞은 표현을 고르세요.

❶

get away ☐

get on ☐

❷

get around ☐

get off ☐

❸

get back ☐

get out of ☐

❹

get into ☐

get over ☐

2 우리말에 알맞게 단어를 배열하여 문장을 완성하세요.

❶ 그녀는 요새 많이 돌아다니지 않는다.

> much ∿ around ∿ get

She doesn't _____ _____ _____ these days.

❷ 너는 몇 시에 돌아올 거야?

> get ∿ you ∿ back

What time will _____ _____ _____?

❸ 지하철에서 내릴 때 발을 조심하세요.

> off ∿ get ∿ the subway

Watch your step when you _____ _____ _____.

❹ 독감에서 회복되길 빌어요.

> the flu ∿ over ∿ get

I hope you _____ _____ _____.

3 그림을 보고 알맞은 문장과 연결하세요.

①

②

③

④

Get out of the building! It is falling apart!

I will get off at the next stop.

He got around by bike.

I am getting into Latin music these days.

4 알맞은 단어를 써서 대화를 완성하세요.

①

A: How was your trip?

B: Good. It was so easy to g_____ _____ by subway.

②

A: Where should I get off the bus?

B: You should g_____ _____ at this stop.

③

A: I'll g_____ _____ home this afternoon.

B: Okay. I'll call you then.

29

get through
통과하다

get through
the doorway
출입구를 통과하다

get together
모이다, 만나다

get together
once a year
1년에 한 번 모이다

---

1 빈칸에 알맞은 구동사를 써보세요.

① 울창한 숲을 통과하다 　　　　　　　　　　　　　 the thick forest

② 연습을 위해 모이다 　　　　　　　　　　　　　 for practice

---

2 빈칸에 알맞은 말을 써서 문장을 완성하세요.

① **First, I have to** 　　　　　　　　　　　　　　　　.

　　우선, 나는 시험을 통과해야만 한다. (the exams)

② **Every week they** 　　　　　　　　　　　　　　　.

　　매주 그들은 음악을 만들기 위해 모인다. (to make music)

---

3 밑줄 친 부분을 우리말 뜻에 맞도록 고쳐보세요.

① **How can we get together the winter?**

　　우리는 어떻게 겨울을 날 수 있을까?

② **Why don't we go together for lunch sometime?**

　　우리 언제 만나서 점심 먹는 게 어때?

---

4 빈칸을 영어로 바꿔보세요.

① **A: Look at that cat!** 저 고양이를 봐!

　　B: Poor thing! _____.

　　불쌍해라! 그는 문을 통과 못 해.

② **A: How often do you meet your friends?** 얼마나 자주 친구들을 만나?

　　B: _____. 우리는 한 달에 한 번 모여.

get up
일어나다

get up at 7:30
7시 30분에 일어나다

get well
회복하다

will get well soon
곧 회복될 것이다

---

1 빈칸에 알맞은 구동사를 써보세요.

① 아침 일찍 일어나다 　　　　　　　　　 early in the morning

② 치료를 하면 회복될 것이다 will 　　　　　　　　 with the treatment

2 빈칸에 알맞은 말을 써서 문장을 완성하세요.

① **My grandfather never** 　　　　　　　　　　　　　　　.

　　우리 할아버지는 일찍 일어나는 데 절대 실패한 적이 없다. (failed to)

② **He must** 　　　　　　　　　　　　　.

　　그는 회복하는 데 스스로 도와야만 한다. (help himself)

3 밑줄 친 부분을 우리말 뜻에 맞도록 고쳐보세요.

① **I sometimes get on late these days.**

　　나는 요새 가끔 늦게 일어난다.

② **I hope you and your family get back soon.**

　　당신과 당신 가족분들이 빨리 회복되기 바라요.

4 빈칸을 영어로 바꿔보세요.

① **A: When do you start your day?** 너는 하루를 언제 시작해?

　　B: _____. 나는 보통 7시에 일어나.

② **A:** _____. **We miss you a lot.** 빨리 회복하세요. 당신이 많이 그리워요.

　　B: Thank you. Let's get together when I get better. 고마워요. 제가 나아지면 한번 만나요.

31

give away
기부하다, 거저 주다

give away
old clothes
헌 옷을 기부하다

give up
포기하다

Don't give up.
포기하지 마.

---

1 빈칸에 알맞은 구동사를 써보세요.

① 돈을 탈탈 털어 기부하다 ⬚⬚ ⬚⬚ her last penny

② 쉽게 포기하다 ⬚⬚ ⬚⬚ easily

---

2 빈칸에 알맞은 말을 써서 문장을 완성하세요.

① I ⬚⬚⬚⬚ to charity.

　나는 쓰던 장난감들을 자선 단체에 기부했다. (old toys)

② She is ⬚⬚⬚⬚.

　그녀는 절대 포기하지 않을 것이다. (never)

---

3 밑줄 친 부분을 우리말 뜻에 맞도록 고쳐보세요.

① We **pass away** our old books to neighbors every year.

　우리는 매년 헌책들을 이웃들에게 나눠 준다.

② I **give out**! I can't find you.

　나 포기할래! 널 찾을 수가 없어.

---

4 빈칸을 영어로 바꿔보세요.

① A: **Your old clothes can be used by us.** 당신의 헌 옷은 우리가 사용할 수 있어요.

　B: I know but ＿＿＿＿＿＿＿＿＿＿ last month.

　　알고 있지만 지난 달에 제 걸 전부 기부했어요.

② A: **Was the test too difficult for you?** 시험이 너한테 너무 어려웠어?

　B: Yes, but ＿＿＿＿＿＿＿＿＿. 응, 하지만 난 포기하지 않았어.

---

go along with
~에 동의하다

go along with his idea
그의 생각에 동의하다

go by
(시간이) 흐르다

Time goes by fast.
시간이 빨리 흐른다.

1 빈칸에 알맞은 구동사를 써보세요.

① 그의 의견에 동의하다 ⬚ ⬚ ⬚ his opinion

② 지난주는 아주 빨리 지나갔다. Last week ⬚ ⬚ so fast.

2 빈칸에 알맞은 말을 써서 문장을 완성하세요.

① I'll ⬚ this time.

나는 이번에는 너한테 동의할게.

② Time ⬚ when you are bored.

지루할 때는 시간이 아주 천천히 흐른다. (slowly)

3 밑줄 친 부분을 우리말 뜻에 맞도록 고쳐보세요.

① I'm afraid I can't <u>get through with</u> her on this matter.

난 이 문제에 대해서 그녀에게 동의할 수 없을 거 같아.

② Things will get better as time <u>goes over</u>.

시간이 지나면 다 잘될 거야.

4 빈칸을 영어로 바꿔보세요.

① A: I won't _____.

나는 프로그램에 대한 그녀의 생각에는 동의하지 않을 거야.

B: I am sorry to hear that. I think it is good for us. 유감이네. 난 그게 우리한테 좋다고 생각하는데.

② A: I'll be a sixth grader next year. 저는 내년에 6학년이 돼요.

B: A sixth grader? _____.

6학년? 시간이 진짜 빨리 지나가네.

1 그림에 알맞은 표현을 고르세요.

❶
get together ☐
give up ☐

❷
get up ☐
get through ☐

❸
get well ☐
give away ☐

❹
go along with ☐
go by ☐

2 우리말에 알맞게 단어를 배열하여 문장을 완성하세요.

❶ 우리는 어떻게 겨울을 날 수 있을까?

the winter ⌇ get ⌇ through

How can we _____ _____ _____?

❷ 그가 약을 먹고 빨리 회복되기를 바라요.

get ⌇ will ⌇ well

I hope he _____ _____ _____ soon with the medicine.

❸ 그녀는 절대 포기하지 않을 것이다.

up ⌇ to ⌇ give

She is never going _____ _____ _____.

❹ 지루할 때는 시간이 아주 천천히 흐른다.

by ⌇ so slowly ⌇ goes

Time _____ _____ _____ when you are bored.

3 그림을 보고 알맞은 문장과 연결하세요.

❶   • • We gave away our old clothes to neighbors.

❷   • • I'll go along with you this time.

❸   • • I get up at 7:30 every day.

❹   • • First, I have to get through the doorway.

4 알맞은 단어를 써서 대화를 완성하세요.

❶

A: How often do you meet your friends?

B: We g_____ _____ once a month.

❷

A: When do you start your day?

B: I usually g_____ _____ at 6:00 in the morning.

❸

A: It is very hard to become a doctor.

B: I know, but I'm never going to g_____ _____.

33

go off (((🔔)))
(경보 등이) 울리다

An alarm goes off.
경보가 울린다.

go over
검토하다, 조사하다

go over plans
계획을 검토하다

---

1 빈칸에 알맞은 구동사를 써보세요.

① 몇 초 동안 (경보가) 울리다 　　　　　　　　 for a few seconds

② 문제를 검토하다 　　　　　　　　 a problem

---

2 빈칸에 알맞은 말을 써서 문장을 완성하세요.

① **The alarm** 　　　　　　　　　　　　　.

알람이 6시에 울린다. (at six)

② **You should** 　　　　　　　　　　　　　 **to find mistakes.**

실수를 발견하려면 네 답들을 검토해야만 한다. (your answers)

---

3 밑줄 친 부분을 우리말 뜻에 맞도록 고쳐보세요.

① **The fire alarm** <u>went through</u> **for no reason.**

화재 경보기가 이유 없이 울렸다.

② **Let's** <u>go by</u> **our schedule.**

우리의 일정을 검토하자.

---

4 빈칸을 영어로 바꿔보세요.

① **A: What are you doing in the house? The fire alarm went off.**

집에서 뭐 하는 중이야? 화재 경보기가 울렸어.

B: It's a false alarm. ＿＿＿＿＿＿＿＿＿＿＿＿. 그거 거짓 경보야. 그게 항상 울려.

② **A:** ＿＿＿＿＿＿＿＿＿＿＿ **before you hand it in.** 제출하기 전에 숙제를 검토하세요.

B: I did twice. 두 번 했어요.

go through
겪다

**go through
a hard time**
어려운 시간을 겪다

grow up
자라다

grow up so quickly
아주 빨리 자라다

---

1 빈칸에 알맞은 구동사를 써보세요.

① 급격한 변화를 겪다 _____ _____ dramatic changes

② 네 아빠처럼 자라다 _____ _____ like your dad

2 빈칸에 알맞은 말을 써서 문장을 완성하세요.

① He is _____.

그는 힘든 시기를 겪고 있다. (a hard time)

② I _____.

나는 시골에서 자랐다. (countryside)

3 밑줄 친 부분을 우리말 뜻에 맞도록 고쳐보세요.

① He is <u>getting through</u> a lot of changes in his life.

그는 인생에서 많은 변화를 겪고 있다.

② Children seem to <u>cover up</u> fast these days.

요즘 아이들은 빨리 자라는 것 같다.

4 빈칸을 영어로 바꿔보세요.

① A: I feel like I can't do anything right these days. 나는 요즘에 아무것도 제대로 못하는 것 같아요.

B: Don't worry. We all _____!

걱정 마. 우리 모두 그 단계를 겪어!

② A: What do you want to be _____? 넌 커서 뭐가 되고 싶어?

B: I want to be a dentist. 난 치과의사가 되고 싶어.

hand down
물려주다

hand down **a necklace**
목걸이를 물려주다

hand in
제출하다

hand in **the report**
보고서를 제출하다

---

1 빈칸에 알맞은 구동사를 써보세요.

① 헌 가구를 물려주다 [   ] [   ] **a piece of old furniture**

② 증거를 경찰에 제출하다 [   ] [   ] **the evidence to the police**

2 빈칸에 알맞은 말을 써서 문장을 완성하세요.

① **Jimmy** [   ] **to his younger brother.**

지미는 자신의 헌 셔츠들을 남동생에게 물려줬다. (old shirts)

② **I** [   ] .

나는 이번에는 숙제를 일찍 제출했다. (this time)

3 밑줄 친 부분을 우리말 뜻에 맞도록 고쳐보세요.

① **My dad handed on his watch to me.**

아빠는 시계를 나한테 물려줬다.

② **Please hand down your essay on time.**

에세이를 정해진 시간에 제출하세요.

4 빈칸을 영어로 바꿔보세요.

① **A:** _____. 언니는 그녀가 입던 옷을 나한테 물려줬어.

B: Don't you just hate that? 그거 싫지 않아?

② **A: What did you do with the money?** 너 그 돈으로 뭐 했어?

B: _____. **Is that okay?** 나 그거 경찰에 제출했어. 괜찮지?

36

hang on to
~을 꽉 붙잡다

hang on to the handle
손잡이를 꽉 붙잡다

hang out with
~와 어울리다

hang out with
friends
친구들과 어울리다

---

1 빈칸에 알맞은 구동사를 써보세요.

① 밧줄을 꽉 잡다 [____] [____] [____] the rope

② 가족들과 어울리다 [____] [____] [____] family

2 빈칸에 알맞은 말을 써서 문장을 완성하세요.

① **It is very windy. Please** [_____].

바람이 많이 부네요. 모자를 꽉 잡으세요. (tightly)

② **I** [_____].

나는 너와 어울리고 싶어. (want to)

3 밑줄 친 부분을 우리말 뜻에 맞도록 고쳐보세요.

① **How long will you hang out with hatred?**

언제까지 그렇게 미워만 할래?

② **The weather was nice, so she hung up with her friends.**

날씨가 좋아서 그녀는 친구들과 어울렸다.

4 빈칸을 영어로 바꿔보세요.

① **A: I want to give up.** 나 포기하고 싶어.

B: No, plaese _____! 아니야, 꿈을 꽉 붙잡으렴!

② **A: What are you going to do this Friday?** 이번주 금요일에 뭐 할 거야?

B: _____ **every Friday.** 난 매주 금요일에 친한 친구들과 어울려.

1 그림에 알맞은 표현을 고르세요.

❶

go off ☐

go over ☐

❷

hand in ☐

hand down ☐

❸

go through ☐

hang out with ☐

❹

hang on to ☐

grow up ☐

2 우리말에 알맞게 단어를 배열하여 문장을 완성하세요.

❶ 우리의 일정을 검토하자.

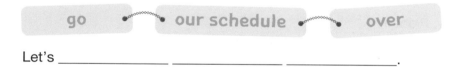

go · · our schedule · · over

Let's ＿＿＿＿＿＿ ＿＿＿＿＿＿ ＿＿＿＿＿＿.

❷ 그는 힘든 시기를 겪고 있다.

going · · through · · is

He ＿＿＿＿＿＿ ＿＿＿＿＿＿ ＿＿＿＿＿＿ a rough patch.

❸ 그녀는 자신의 헌 셔츠들을 여동생에게 물려줬다.

down · · her old shirts · · handed

She ＿＿＿＿＿＿ ＿＿＿＿＿＿ ＿＿＿＿＿＿ to her younger sister.

❹ 나는 너랑 어울리고 싶어.

out · · hang · · with

I want to ＿＿＿＿＿＿ ＿＿＿＿＿＿ ＿＿＿＿＿＿ you.

3 그림을 보고 알맞은 문장과 연결하세요.

① • • Children grow up so quickly.

② • • Please hang on to the handle.

③ • • The fire alarm went off for no reason.

④ • • I handed in the report early this time.

4 알맞은 단어를 써서 대화를 완성하세요.

①

A: What is that sound?

B: OMG. The fire alarm w_____ _____.
Let's go outside.

②

A: What do you want to be when you g_____ _____?

B: I want to be a scientist.

③

A: What are you going to do this Friday?

B: I h_____ _____ _____ my best friend every
Friday.

hang up
전화를 끊다

hang up now
지금 전화를 끊다

hold back
(감정 등을) 참다, 비밀로 하다

hold back tears
눈물을 참다

---

1 빈칸에 알맞은 구동사를 써보세요.

① 전화를 끊어주세요.   _____ _____, please.

② 트림을 참다   _____ _____ a burp

2 빈칸에 알맞은 말을 써서 문장을 완성하세요.

① **Don't** _____. I need to talk to you.

내 전화 끊지 마. 너한테 할말 있어. (on me)

② **Do not** _____.

진실을 감추지 마. (the truth)

3 밑줄 친 부분을 우리말 뜻에 맞도록 고쳐보세요.

① **Please hang on. I'll call you back.**

전화를 끊어 주세요. 제가 다시 전화드릴게요.

② **It is difficult to call back anger sometimes.**

가끔씩 화를 참는 게 어렵다.

4 빈칸을 영어로 바꿔보세요.

① A: Oh, _____. My mom is calling me.

아, 지금 전화 끊어야겠어. 엄마가 나를 부르고 계셔.

B: Okay. You'd better answer that! 알았어. 너는 대답을 하는 게 좋겠어!

② A: The story was so funny! 그 이야기는 너무 웃겼어!

B: Absolutely. _____. 정말 그래. 나는 웃음을 참을 수 없더라고.

38

hold on
기다리다

hold on a second
잠시 기다리다

hold out
내밀다

hold out your arms
팔을 뻗다

---

1 빈칸에 알맞은 구동사를 써보세요.

① 잠깐 기다려주세요.　　　　**Please** ＿＿＿＿ ＿＿＿＿ **a minute.**

② 표를 내밀다　　　　＿＿＿＿ ＿＿＿＿ **the ticket**

2 빈칸에 알맞은 말을 써서 문장을 완성하세요.

① **Do you wish to** ＿＿＿＿＿＿＿＿＿＿**?**

　다시 거시겠어요? 아니면 기다리시겠습니까? (call back)

② **Please** ＿＿＿＿＿＿＿＿＿**.**

　손을 내밀어주세요. (your hand)

3 밑줄 친 부분을 우리말 뜻에 맞도록 고쳐보세요.

① **Could you please** <u>hold up</u> **for a while?**

　잠시만 기다려주시겠어요?

② **He** <u>held on</u> **the microphone to me.**

　그는 마이크를 나한테 내밀었다.

4 빈칸을 영어로 바꿔보세요.

① **A: Do you want me to give you the phone number?** 전화번호를 알려줄까?

　B: ＿＿＿＿＿＿＿＿＿＿**. I need a pen and paper.** 잠깐 기다려. 펜과 종이를 준비할게.

② **A: I've got something for you.** ＿＿＿＿＿＿＿＿＿＿**.** 나 너한테 줄 게 있어. 손 내밀어봐.

　B: Ohhh… I'm excited! 오, 기대가 되는데!

39

hold up
들고 있다

hold up one's hands
손을 들고 있다

hurry up
서두르다

Hurry up, please.
서둘러 주세요.

---

1 빈칸에 알맞은 구동사를 써보세요.

① 카메라를 들고 있다   **the camera**

② 커피를 빨리 마시다   **with the coffee**

2 빈칸에 알맞은 말을 써서 문장을 완성하세요.

① ＿＿＿＿＿＿＿＿＿＿＿＿＿＿＿＿＿＿＿＿ **so I can see what's in them.**

손을 들고 있어 보세요, 그 안에 뭐가 있는지 볼 수 있게요. (your hands)

② ＿＿＿＿＿＿＿＿＿＿＿＿＿＿＿＿＿＿＿＿ **.**

서둘러, 그렇지 않으면 지각할 거야. (be late)

3 밑줄 친 부분을 우리말 뜻에 맞도록 고쳐보세요.

① **He will** <u>hold back</u> **the sign for you to see.**

그는 네가 볼 수 있게 보드를 들고 있을 거야.

② **We don't have time. We should** <u>cheer up</u>**.**

시간이 없어. 우리는 서둘러야 해.

4 빈칸을 영어로 바꿔보세요.

① **A: I have a question!** 저 질문 있어요!

   B: Please ＿＿＿＿＿＿＿＿＿＿＿＿＿＿＿ if you have any questions.

     질문이 있으시면 손을 들어주세요.

② **A: Are we going out?** 우리 외출해?

   B: Yes, so ＿＿＿＿＿＿＿＿＿ and get dressed! 응, 그러니까 서둘러 옷 입어!

leave for
~로 떠나다

leave for England
영국으로 떠나다

let (someone) down
(~를) 실망시키다

let him down
그를 실망시키다

---

1 빈칸에 알맞은 구동사를 써보세요.

① 공항으로 떠나다   the airport

② 나를 실망시키지 마.   Don't   me   .

2 빈칸에 알맞은 말을 써서 문장을 완성하세요.

① **Don't forget the camera before** _____.

여행 떠나기 전에 카메라 잊지 마. (the trip)

② **I hope he won't** _____.

그가 팬들을 실망시키지 않기를 바라. (his fans)

3 밑줄 친 부분을 우리말 뜻에 맞도록 고쳐보세요.

① **When do you live for work?**

언제 일하러 가?

② **I'm sorry for letting my parents out.**

부모님을 실망시켜드려서 죄송해요.

4 빈칸을 영어로 바꿔보세요.

① **A: Are you going somewhere?** 너 어디 가니?

B: You didn't know? I'm _____. 너 몰랐어? 나 프랑스로 떠날 거야.

② **A: I'm sorry for** _____.

시험 결과로 실망시켜서 죄송해요.

B: That's okay. You can try harder next time. 괜찮아. 다음 번에 더 열심히 하면 되지.

1 그림에 알맞은 표현을 고르세요.

① hold back ☐
hold out ☐

② let down ☐
hang up ☐

③ hold on ☐
hurry up ☐

④ leave for ☐
hold up ☐

2 우리말에 알맞게 단어를 배열하여 문장을 완성하세요.

① 진실을 감추지 마.

the truth　back　hold

Do not ＿＿＿＿ ＿＿＿＿ ＿＿＿＿.

② 잠깐 기다려주시겠어요?

on　please　hold

Could you ＿＿＿＿ ＿＿＿＿, ＿＿＿＿?

③ 그녀는 네가 볼 수 있게 보드를 들고 있을 거야.

hold　the sign　up

She will ＿＿＿＿ ＿＿＿＿ ＿＿＿＿ for you to see.

④ 나는 그가 부모님을 실망시키시지 않기를 바라.

his parents　down　let

I hope he won't ＿＿＿＿ ＿＿＿＿ ＿＿＿＿.

3 그림을 보고 알맞은 문장과 연결하세요.

❶

We don't have time. We should hurry up.

❷

He held out his arms to me.

❸

Please hang up now. I'll call you back.

❹

I am going to leave for America.

4 알맞은 단어를 써서 대화를 완성하세요.

❶

A: The story was so funny!

B: Absolutely. I couldn't h_____ _____ my laughter.

❷

A: Do you want me to give you the email address?

B: H_____ _____ a second. I need a pen and paper.

❸

A: I'm sorry for l_____ you _____.

B: That's okay. You can try harder next time.

let out
(소리, 한숨 등을) 쉬다

let out a deep sigh
깊은 한숨을 쉬다

lie down
눕다

lie down on the bed
침대에 눕다

---

1 빈칸에 알맞은 구동사를 써보세요.

① 고통스러운 비명을 지르다 [_____] [_____] a scream of pain

② 강아지들과 눕다 [_____] [_____] with the dogs

2 빈칸에 알맞은 말을 써서 문장을 완성하세요.

① He [_____].

그는 불신의 비명을 질렀다. (a cry of disbelief)

② Why don't you [_____]?

누워서 쉬는 게 어때? (relax)

3 밑줄 친 부분을 우리말 뜻에 맞도록 고쳐보세요.

① He <u>went out</u> a loud sneeze.

그는 크게 재채기를 했다.

② I feel dizzy and need to <u>let down</u> for a second.

나 어지러워서 잠깐 누워야겠어.

4 빈칸을 영어로 바꿔보세요.

① A: Did Sarah get hurt? 사라가 다쳤어?

B: Yes, she _____ when she got hurt. 응, 그녀는 다쳤을 때 비명을 질렀어.

② A: Where's Charlie? 찰리는 어디 있지?

B: He went to _____ after the long trip. 긴 여행을 마친 후라서 그는 누우러 갔어.

42

line up
줄을 서다

line up in a row
한 줄로 서다

long for
간절히 바라다

long for fine weather
좋은 날씨를 간절히 바라다

1 빈칸에 알맞은 구동사를 써보세요.

① 얘들아, 줄 서.
　　　　　　　　　　　　　, children.

② 더 조용한 삶을 바라다
　　　　　　　　　　　　　a quieter life

2 빈칸에 알맞은 말을 써서 문장을 완성하세요.

① **People should** _____.
경기장에 입장하려면 줄을 서야 한다. (enter the stadium)

② **He** _____.
그는 아빠의 조언을 간절히 바랐다. (advice)

3 밑줄 친 부분을 우리말 뜻에 맞도록 고쳐보세요.

① **A lot of fans covered up for photos and autographs.**
수많은 팬들이 사진을 찍고 사인을 받으려고 줄을 섰다.

② **We go for a trip to Italy for our next vacation.**
우리는 다음 휴가 때 이탈리아로 여행 가기를 간절히 바란다.

4 빈칸을 영어로 바꿔보세요.

① **A: It's lunch time!** 점심 시간이다!

   B: _____, **children.** 얘들아, 문 앞에 줄을 서렴.

② **A: I** _____! 시원한 바람이 불었으면 좋겠어!

   B: I do, too. It's been too hot these days. 나도 그래. 요즘 너무 더웠어.

43

look after
보살피다

look after
the children
아이들을 보살피다

look around
둘러보다

look around
a new school
새 학교를 둘러보다

1 빈칸에 알맞은 구동사를 써보세요.

① 그녀의 햄스터를 보살피다 ⬜⬜ ⬜⬜ her hamster

② 구 시가지를 둘러보다 ⬜⬜ ⬜⬜ the old town

2 빈칸에 알맞은 말을 써서 문장을 완성하세요.

① I'll ⬜⬜⬜⬜ when you're gone.

당신이 떠나 있는 동안 내가 당신 아기를 보살필게요. (your baby)

② **What is the best way to** ⬜⬜⬜⬜ ?

도시를 둘러보는 가장 좋은 방법이 뭐예요? (the city)

3 밑줄 친 부분을 우리말 뜻에 맞도록 고쳐보세요.

① **She takes after homeless dogs.**

그녀는 집 없는 개들을 보살핀다.

② **How about nosing around the park after lunch?**

점심 먹은 후에 공원을 둘러보는 게 어때?

4 빈칸을 영어로 바꿔보세요.

① A: Look at the little girl! _____.

어린 소녀를 봐봐! 그녀는 어린 남동생을 보살피고 있어.

B: Yes, they look so cute! 응, 쟤들 너무 귀여워!

② A: What shall we do after lunch? 점심 먹고 나서 뭐 할까?

B: We can _____.What do you think?

우리는 도시를 둘러볼 수 있을 거 같아. 어떻게 생각해?

44

look for
찾다

look for **a needle**
바늘을 찾다

look forward to
고대하다

look forward to **the winter vacation** 겨울 방학을 고대하다

---

1 빈칸에 알맞은 구동사를 써보세요.

① 가장 가까운 지하철역을 찾다 ⬜⬜ **the nearest subway station**

② 당신의 연락을 기다리다 ⬜⬜⬜ **hearing from you**

2 빈칸에 알맞은 말을 써서 문장을 완성하세요.

① **She's** ⬜⬜⬜⬜ **.**

그녀는 자동차 열쇠를 찾고 있다. (her car key)

② **They're** ⬜⬜⬜⬜ **.**

그들은 당신의 방문을 고대하고 있어요. (your visit)

3 밑줄 친 부분을 우리말 뜻에 맞도록 고쳐보세요.

① **I cared for my dog for an hour.**

나는 한 시간 동안 우리 개를 찾았다.

② **I am really looking up to his concert.**

나는 간절히 그의 콘서트를 기대하고 있다.

4 빈칸을 영어로 바꿔보세요.

① **A:** _____**?** 너 뭐 찾고 있어?

B: I'm looking for my phone. Have you seen it? 내 전화기를 찾고 있어. 그거 본 적 있니?

② **A: It's great to finally meet you.** 마침내 당신을 만나서 기쁘네요.

B: _____**.** 저도 만나뵙기를 기대하고 있었어요.

Review

1 그림에 알맞은 표현을 고르세요.

①

②

③

④

lie down ☐   line up ☐   look for ☐   look forward to ☐

long for ☐   look after ☐   let out ☐   look around ☐

2 우리말에 알맞게 단어를 배열하여 문장을 완성하세요.

① 나는 내 이어폰을 찾고 있다.

for ～ looking ～ my earphones

I'm _____ _____ _____.

② 누워서 쉬는 게 어때요?

down ～ lie ～ you

Why don't _____ _____ _____ and relax?

③ 그 소년은 집 잃은 고양이들을 보살폈다.

after ～ looked ～ homeless cats

The boy _____ _____ _____.

④ 수많은 사람들이 한 줄로 서 있었다.

lined ～ up ～ people

A lot of _____ _____ _____ in a row.

3 그림을 보고 알맞은 문장과 연결하세요.

❶
•　　　•　He let out a deep sigh.

❷
•　　　•　People should line up to enter the stadium.

❸
•　　　•　He's looking for a needle.

❹
•　　　•　I'll look around my new school.

4 알맞은 단어를 써서 대화를 완성하세요.

❶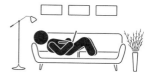

A: Where is Lucas?

B: He is l_____ _____ on the sofa.

❷

A: It's too hot this summer.

B: You're right. I l_____ _____ a cool breeze!

❸

A: Can you l_____ _____ my hamster until Monday?

B: Sure, I have enough time on the weekend.

45

look into
조사하다

look into the matter
그 문제를 조사하다

look up to
존경하다

look up to her parents
그녀의 부모를 존경하다

---

1 빈칸에 알맞은 구동사를 써보세요.

① 문제를 조사하다 ⬚⬚ ⬚⬚ **the problem**

② 전설적인 감독을 존경하다 ⬚⬚ ⬚⬚ ⬚⬚ **the legendary director**

2 빈칸에 알맞은 말을 써서 문장을 완성하세요.

① **The police** ⬚⬚⬚⬚ .

경찰은 사고 원인을 조사했다. (the cause of the accident)

② **They all** ⬚⬚⬚⬚ .

그들 모두 그들의 선생님을 존경한다. (their teacher)

3 밑줄 친 부분을 우리말 뜻에 맞도록 고쳐보세요.

① I'll <u>look after</u> the reasons for the decision.

나는 그 결정의 이유를 조사할 거야.

② We <u>look forward to</u> him as a hero.

우리는 그를 영웅처럼 우러러본다.

4 빈칸을 영어로 바꿔보세요.

① A: Did you hear about the accident on the news? 뉴스에 나온 사고에 대해 들었어?

B: Yes, ＿＿＿＿＿＿＿＿＿＿ in detail. 응, 경찰이 자세히 조사하고 있어.

② A: Who do you look up to the most? 넌 누구를 가장 존경하니?

B: ＿＿＿＿＿＿＿＿＿＿. 나는 우리 아빠를 가장 존경해.

make out
이해하다, 알아보다

make out his handwriting
그의 손글씨를 알아보다

make up
지어내다

make up a story
이야기를 지어내다

---

1 빈칸에 알맞은 구동사를 써보세요.

① 사진에 있는 사람을 알아보다 ⬚ ⬚ **a person in the photo**

② 이유를 둘러대다 ⬚ ⬚ **an excuse**

2 빈칸에 알맞은 말을 써서 문장을 완성하세요.

① **I can't** ⬚ **.**

그의 편지 마지막 부분을 알아볼 수 없다. (the last part of his letter)

② **Did you** ⬚ **yourself?**

그 이야기를 네가 직접 지어낸 거야? (the story)

3 밑줄 친 부분을 우리말 뜻에 맞도록 고쳐보세요.

① **I cannot hold out the last two words on the poster.**

나는 포스터에 있는 마지막 두 단어를 알아볼 수 없다.

② **We need to mess up short dialogues for the play.**

우리는 연극에 쓸 짧은 대화문을 지어내야 한다.

4 빈칸을 영어로 바꿔보세요.

① **A: Can you read the letters?** 너 저 글자들을 읽을 수 있어?

B: _____ because they are so tiny. 글자가 너무 작아서 알아볼 수 없어.

② **A: Honestly, I didn't _____!** 솔직히, 내가 그 이야기를 지어낸 것은 아니야!

B: Well, I still don't believe you. 글쎄, 난 여전히 너 안 믿어.

mess up
엉망으로
만들어 버리다
mess up a room
방을 어지르다

nose out
찾아내다
nose out a scandal
소문을 알아내다

---

1 빈칸에 알맞은 구동사를 써보세요.

① 내 머리를 헝클다 _____ _____ my hair

② 그의 친구의 비밀을 알아내다 _____ _____ his friend's secrets

2 빈칸에 알맞은 말을 써서 문장을 완성하세요.

① **The reporter** _____.

그 기자는 그녀의 명성을 망쳤다. (her reputation)

② **My dog can** _____.

우리 강아지는 어디에서든 자신의 간식을 찾아낼 수 있다. (his treats anywhere)

3 밑줄 친 부분을 우리말 뜻에 맞도록 고쳐보세요.

① **Your cat <u>made up</u> my shoes!**

네 고양이가 내 구두를 엉망으로 만들었어!

② **He <u>picked out</u> the details by talking to people.**

그는 사람들과 얘기하면서 세부적인 내용을 알아냈다.

4 빈칸을 영어로 바꿔보세요.

① **A: Mom, _____!** 엄마, 토미가 내 머리를 망치고 있어요!

B: Don't mess up your sister's hair, Tommy! 누나 머리 망치면 안돼, 토미!

② **A: That reporter always _____.** 그 기자는 항상 뉴스거리를 찾아.

B: I know. How does he do that? 그러게. 그는 그걸 어떻게 하는 걸까?

48

part with
~와 헤어지다

part with his children
during the war
전쟁 때 아이들과 헤어지다

pass away
돌아가시다

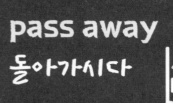

suddenly pass away
갑자기 돌아가시다

---

1 빈칸에 알맞은 구동사를 써보세요.

① 그녀의 딸과 헤어지다 ⬚⬚⬚ ⬚⬚⬚ her daughter

② 곧 돌아가시다 ⬚⬚⬚ ⬚⬚⬚ soon

2 빈칸에 알맞은 말을 써서 문장을 완성하세요.

① **I don't want to** ⬚⬚⬚⬚⬚ .

나는 내 친구 누구와도 헤어지고 싶지 않다. (any of my friends)

② **My grandmother** ⬚⬚⬚⬚⬚ .

우리 할머니는 작년에 돌아가셨다. (last year)

3 밑줄 친 부분을 우리말 뜻에 맞도록 고쳐보세요.

① **I just couldn't get into my old car.**

나는 내 오래된 차와 헤어질 수가 없었다.

② **The patient passed by peacefully at home.**

그 환자는 집에서 평화롭게 돌아가셨다.

4 빈칸을 영어로 바꿔보세요.

① **A: That blanket is very dirty and old. Throw it out.** 그 담요는 너무 더럽고 오래됐어. 버려.

B: _____, **Mom! Not yet!** 내 담요를 버릴 수 없어요, 엄마! 아직은 안 돼요!

② **A: Do you have a grandfather?** 너는 할아버지가 계시니?

B: _____**when I was young.** 우리 할아버지는 내가 어렸을 때 돌아가셨어.

1 그림에 알맞은 표현을 고르세요.

①

look up to ☐

mess up ☐

②

make out ☐

look into ☐

③

make up ☐

pass away ☐

④

part with ☐

nose out ☐

2 우리말에 알맞게 단어를 배열하여 문장을 완성하세요.

① 그 기자는 그녀의 명성을 망쳤다.

up ∼ messed ∼ her reputation

The reporter ＿＿＿＿＿＿ ＿＿＿＿＿＿ ＿＿＿＿＿＿.

② 그는 이유를 둘러댔다.

up ∼ an excuse ∼ made

He ＿＿＿＿＿＿ ＿＿＿＿＿＿ ＿＿＿＿＿＿.

③ 그녀는 사고를 조사하고 있다.

the accident ∼ into ∼ looking

She is ＿＿＿＿＿＿ ＿＿＿＿＿＿ ＿＿＿＿＿＿.

④ 나는 친한 친구와 헤어지고 싶지 않다.

with ∼ part ∼ my best friend

I don't want to ＿＿＿＿＿＿ ＿＿＿＿＿＿ ＿＿＿＿＿＿.

3 그림을 보고 알맞은 문장과 연결하세요.

❶ • • He parted with his children during the war.

❷ • • When did you make up the story?

❸ • • He looked into the matter.

❹ • • My dog messed up my room when I went out.

4 알맞은 단어를 써서 대화를 완성하세요.

❶

A: Who do you look up to the most?

B: I / _____ _____ _____ my father the most.

❷

A: Can you read her handwriting?

B: No. I can't m_____ _____ the letters because they are so tiny.

❸

A: Do you have a grandfather?

B: My grandfather p_____ _____ when I was young.

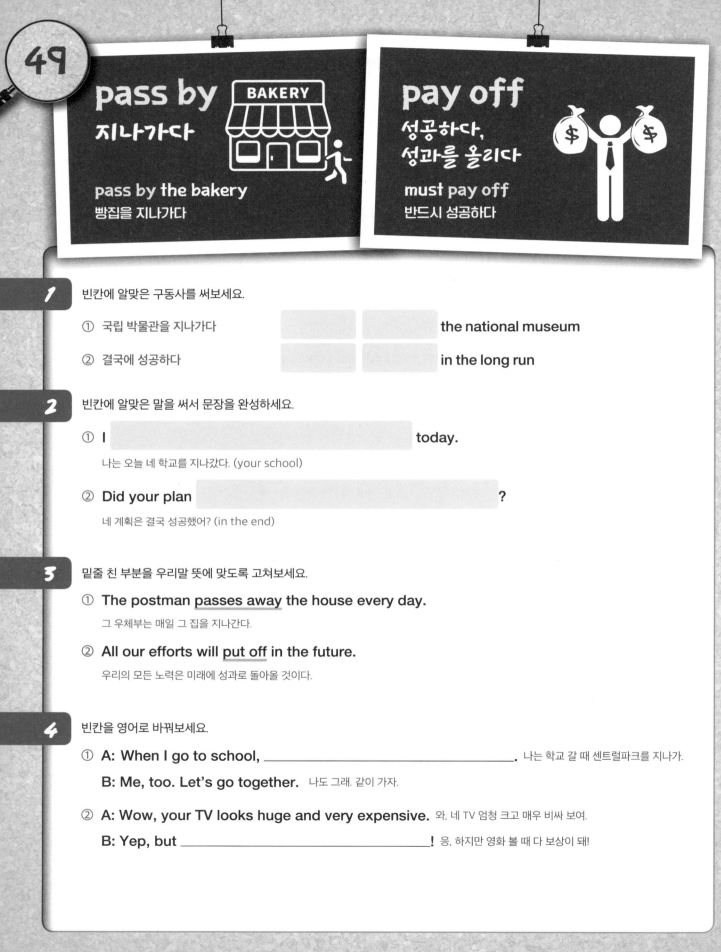

49

pass by
지나가다

pass by the bakery
빵집을 지나가다

pay off
성공하다,
성과를 올리다

must pay off
반드시 성공하다

---

1 빈칸에 알맞은 구동사를 써보세요.

① 국립 박물관을 지나가다 [   ] [   ] the national museum

② 결국에 성공하다 [   ] [   ] in the long run

---

2 빈칸에 알맞은 말을 써서 문장을 완성하세요.

① I [   ] today.

나는 오늘 네 학교를 지나갔다. (your school)

② **Did your plan** [   ] ?

네 계획은 결국 성공했어? (in the end)

---

3 밑줄 친 부분을 우리말 뜻에 맞도록 고쳐보세요.

① **The postman passes away the house every day.**

그 우체부는 매일 그 집을 지나간다.

② **All our efforts will put off in the future.**

우리의 모든 노력은 미래에 성과로 돌아올 것이다.

---

4 빈칸을 영어로 바꿔보세요.

① **A: When I go to school, _____.** 나는 학교 갈 때 센트럴파크를 지나가.

B: Me, too. Let's go together. 나도 그래. 같이 가자.

② **A: Wow, your TV looks huge and very expensive.** 와, 네 TV 엄청 크고 매우 비싸 보여.

B: Yep, but _____! 응, 하지만 영화 볼 때 다 보상이 돼!

pick out
고르다

pick out a gift
선물을 고르다

pick up
가서 태우다

pick him up
그를 태워 오다

1 빈칸에 알맞은 구동사를 써보세요.

① 신선한 야채를 고르다 ☐ ☐ fresh vegetables

② 학교에서 제니를 데리고 오다 ☐ ☐ Jenny from school

2 빈칸에 알맞은 말을 써서 문장을 완성하세요.

① **You can** ☐ .
너는 목록에서 두 개의 장난감을 고를 수 있다. (two toys)

② **I** ☐ .
나는 그를 도서관에 가서 태워 왔다. (from the library)

3 밑줄 친 부분을 우리말 뜻에 맞도록 고쳐보세요.

① **I picked up my mom's birthday invitation card.**
나는 우리 엄마의 생일 초대 카드를 골랐다.

② **He packed her up from the library.**
그는 그녀를 도서관에 가서 태워 왔다.

4 빈칸을 영어로 바꿔보세요.

① **A: I am going to a party tomorrow.** 나는 내일 파티에 갈 거야.

B: _____ **then?** 그러면 드레스 고르는 데 내 도움이 필요하니?

② **A: How will Tom get home?** 톰은 어떻게 집에 와?

B: _____ **.** 내가 그를 학교 가서 태워 올게.

point out
가리키다, 지적하다

point out errors
실수를 지적하다

pop up
갑자기 나타나다

pop up in mind
마음 속에 떠오르다

1 빈칸에 알맞은 구동사를 써보세요.

① 약점을 지적하다 ⬜⬜ ⬜⬜ **weakness**

② 어디에서든 나타나다 ⬜⬜ ⬜⬜ **at every corner**

2 빈칸에 알맞은 말을 써서 문장을 완성하세요.

① **I'd like to** ⬜⬜⬜ **.**

저는 한 가지를 지적하고 싶습니다. (one thing)

② **A lot of cafés are** ⬜⬜⬜ **.**

현재 많은 카페들이 생겨나고 있다. (now)

3 밑줄 친 부분을 우리말 뜻에 맞도록 고쳐보세요.

① **She came out the benefits of eating breakfast.**

그녀는 아침을 먹는 것의 장점을 언급했다.

② **He always holds up at the most inconvenient time.**

그는 항상 가장 불편한 시간에 나타난다.

4 빈칸을 영어로 바꿔보세요.

① **A: Why isn't he** _____? 그는 왜 그들의 실수를 지적하지 않는 거죠?

B: He doesn't care much about other people. 그는 다른 사람들에 대해 크게 신경 쓰지 않아요.

② **A: Your robot vacuum is quiet.** 너의 로봇 진공 청소기는 조용하네.

B: Yeah, but it _____ **and makes me jump.**

응, 하지만 그것이 가끔씩 갑자기 나타나서 나를 펄쩍 뛰게 해.

pull up
멈추다

pull up at the traffic lights
신호등에서 멈추다

put off
연기하다

put off departure
출발을 연기하다

---

1 빈칸에 알맞은 구동사를 써보세요.

① 주유소에서 멈추다 　　　　　　　　　　 **at a gas station**

② 파티를 연기하다 　　　　　　　　　 **the party**

2 빈칸에 알맞은 말을 써서 문장을 완성하세요.

① **The taxi** 　　　　　　　　　　　　　　　　　**.**

　　택시는 입구에 멈췄다. (at the entrance)

② **Can I** 　　　　　　　　　　　　　　　　**?**

　　회의를 연기할 수 있을까요? (the meeting)

3 밑줄 친 부분을 우리말 뜻에 맞도록 고쳐보세요.

① **Please put up in front of the subway station.**

　　지하철역 앞에서 세워주세요.

② **Don't get off today's work!**

　　오늘 할 일을 미루지 마!

4 빈칸을 영어로 바꿔보세요.

① **A: A suspicious black SUV** ＿＿＿＿＿＿＿＿＿＿＿＿＿**.** 의심스러운 검정색 SUV가 우리 뒤에 멈췄어.

　　B: Whooo, maybe they are spies or gangsters! 오, 그들은 아마도 첩자나 불량배일 거야!

② **A: Don't** ＿＿＿＿＿＿＿＿＿＿＿＿＿＿**.** 네 숙제를 내일로 미루지 마.

　　B: Yes, Mom. I'll do it today. 알아요, 엄마. 오늘 할 거예요.

1 그림에 알맞은 표현을 고르세요.

pass by ☐	pay off ☐	point out ☐	put off ☐
pop up ☐	pull up ☐	pick up ☐	pick out ☐

2 우리말에 알맞게 단어를 배열하여 문장을 완성하세요.

❶ 나는 신선한 야채를 고를 수 있다.

I _____ _____ _____ fresh vegetables.

❷ 그 배달부는 매일 내 아파트를 지나간다.

The delivery man _____ _____ _____ every day.

❸ 그는 달리기의 장점을 언급했다.

He _____ _____ _____ of running.

❹ 버스 정류장 앞에서 세워주세요.

_____ _____ _____ in front of the bus stop.

3 그림을 보고 알맞은 문장과 연결하세요.

❶   • • The car pulled up at the entrance.

❷ • • I passed by the bakery today.

❸ • • Is it okay to point out errors?

❹ • • Can you help me pick out a gift?

4 알맞은 단어를 써서 대화를 완성하세요.

❶
A: When I go to the library, I p_____ _____ Central Park.
B: Oh, really? Let's go together.

❷
A: How will you get home?
B: My mom will p_____ me _____ from school.

❸
A: Don't p_____ _____ today's work until tomorrow.
B: Okay, Dad! I'll clean my room right now.

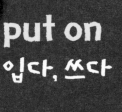

53

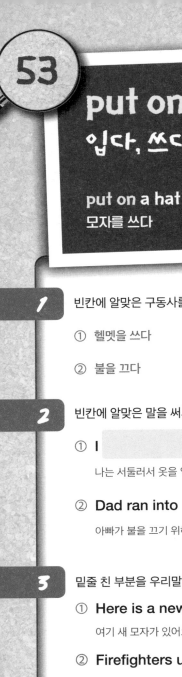

put on
입다, 쓰다
put on a hat
모자를 쓰다

put out
불을 끄다

put out a fire
불을 끄다

---

1 빈칸에 알맞은 구동사를 써보세요.

① 헬멧을 쓰다 ⬚⬚⬚ ⬚⬚⬚ a helmet

② 불을 끄다 ⬚⬚⬚ ⬚⬚⬚ the blaze

2 빈칸에 알맞은 말을 써서 문장을 완성하세요.

① I ⬚⬚⬚⬚⬚⬚⬚ in a hurry.

나는 서둘러서 옷을 입었다. (my clothes)

② Dad ran into the kitchen to ⬚⬚⬚⬚⬚⬚ .

아빠가 불을 끄기 위해 부엌에 뛰어 들어가셨다. (the fire)

3 밑줄 친 부분을 우리말 뜻에 맞도록 고쳐보세요.

① Here is a new hat. Please <u>put it out</u>.

여기 새 모자가 있어요. 그것을 써보세요.

② Firefighters use a huge amount of water to <u>go out</u> fires.

소방관들은 불을 끄기 위해 엄청난 양의 물을 사용한다.

4 빈칸을 영어로 바꿔보세요.

① A: Mom, I'm going to school. 엄마, 저 학교 갈게요.

B: Before you go out, _____. 나가기 전에 재킷 꼭 입어야 돼.

② A: _____. 소방관들이 불을 끄고 있어.

B: Yes, did you see their special hoses? They're really massive!

그러게, 그들이 쓰는 특수 호스 봤어? 그것들은 정말 크네!

put up
올리다, 게시하다,
설치하다

put up a flag
깃발을 올리다

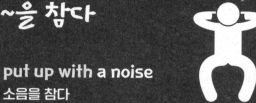

put up with
~을 참다

put up with a noise
소음을 참다

---

1 빈칸에 알맞은 구동사를 써보세요.

① 공지를 게시하다 　　　　　　　　　　　 a notice

② 그의 무례한 행동을 참다 　　　　　　　　　　　　 his rude behavior

2 빈칸에 알맞은 말을 써서 문장을 완성하세요.

① I 　　　　　　　　　　　　　　　　.

　나는 우산을 폈다. (my umbrella)

② The teacher doesn't 　　　　　　　　　　　　.

　그 선생님은 학생들의 지각을 참지 못한다. (students' lateness)

3 밑줄 친 부분을 우리말 뜻에 맞도록 고쳐보세요.

① Bob <u>put out</u> posters on the walls of the office.

　밥은 사무실 벽들에 포스터들을 게시했다.

② I can't <u>hang out with</u> bad manners in classroom.

　나는 교실에서의 버릇없는 태도를 참을 수 없다.

4 빈칸을 영어로 바꿔보세요.

① A: ＿＿＿＿＿＿＿＿＿＿＿＿＿＿＿＿＿? 나를 위해 커튼을 달아줄 수 있어?

　B: Sure. Where do you want them? 그럼. 어디에 달기를 원해?

② A: My neighbors are always chatting outside my door.

　　내 이웃들은 항상 내 집 문밖에서 수다를 떨고 있어.

　B: ＿＿＿＿＿＿＿＿＿＿＿＿＿＿＿＿? 그걸 어떻게 참아?

55

rely on
믿다, 의존하다

rely on me
나를 믿다

rule out
제외시키다

rule out the possibility
가능성을 배제하다

---

1 빈칸에 알맞은 구동사를 써보세요.

① 천연가스에 의존하다   ☐☐☐   ☐☐☐ natural gas

② 나쁜 선택들을 제외하다   ☐☐☐   ☐☐☐ the bad options

2 빈칸에 알맞은 말을 써서 문장을 완성하세요.

① **We should** ☐☐☐☐☐☐☐☐ **in the future.**

우리는 미래에 친환경 에너지에 의존해야만 한다. (green energy)

② **We can't** ☐☐☐☐☐☐☐☐ **in the universe.**

우리는 우주에 다른 생명체가 존재함을 배제할 수 없다. (the existence of other life)

3 밑줄 친 부분을 우리말 뜻에 맞도록 고쳐보세요.

① **Many people put on the Internet for getting information.**

많은 사람들은 정보를 얻기 위해 인터넷에 의존한다.

② **His age points him out as a candidate for President.**

그는 나이 때문에 대통령 후보에서 제외된다.

4 빈칸을 영어로 바꿔보세요.

① **A: Parents are important.** 부모는 중요해요.

B: Indeed, as children we _____ **for everything.**

그렇고말고요, 아이 때에는 우리는 모든 것을 부모님께 의존하잖아요.

② **A:** _____ **because it was too expensive.**

그 해결책은 비싸기 때문에 제외됐어요.

B: Too bad. I will come up with a new idea. 애석하네요. 새로운 아이디어를 낼게요.

---

run after
~을 뒤쫓다

run after a rabbit
토끼를 쫓다

run away
도망치다

run away from danger
위험에서 도망치다

1 빈칸에 알맞은 구동사를 써보세요.

① 버스를 쫓아가다 ⬜⬜ ⬜⬜ the bus

② 집에서 도망치다 ⬜⬜ ⬜⬜ from home

2 빈칸에 알맞은 말을 써서 문장을 완성하세요.

① **A policeman** ⬜⬜⬜ **from 100 meters behind.**

한 경찰관이 100미터 뒤에서 도둑을 쫓고 있었다. (a thief)

② **He just** ⬜⬜⬜ **.**

그는 그냥 도망쳐서 숨기를 원했다. (hide)

3 밑줄 친 부분을 우리말 뜻에 맞도록 고쳐보세요.

① **She looked after the bus as it drove away.**

그녀는 떠나고 있는 버스를 쫓아갔다.

② **You can't just take away from the situation.**

너는 그 상황에서 그냥 도망칠 순 없다.

4 빈칸을 영어로 바꿔보세요.

① **A: What is happening over there?** 저쪽에 무슨 일이 있어?

B: Some dogs are _____. 몇몇 개들이 여우를 쫓고 있어.

② **A: Where is he?** 그는 어디 있어?

B: He saw a wild bear and _____. 그는 야생 곰을 보고 도망쳤어.

1 그림에 알맞은 표현을 고르세요.

❶ put on ☐
put up with ☐

❷ run away ☐
put up ☐

❸ run after ☐
put out ☐

❹ rely on ☐
rule out ☐

2 우리말에 알맞게 단어를 배열하여 문장을 완성하세요.

❶ 나는 깃발을 올렸다.

up   the flag   put

I _____ _____ _____.

❷ 재킷 꼭 입어야 해.

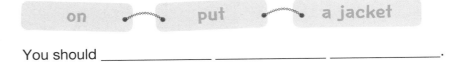

on   put   a jacket

You should _____ _____ _____.

❸ 한 소년이 버스를 쫓아가고 있다.

after   running   the bus

A boy is _____ _____ _____.

❹ 많은 사람들은 정보를 얻기 위해 인터넷에 의존한다.

the Internet   on   rely

Many people _____ _____ _____ for getting information.

3 그림을 보고 알맞은 문장과 연결하세요.

❶ • • He put up a flag in front of his school.

❷ • • We should rely on green energy in the future.

❸ • • A dog is running after a rabbit.

❹  • • I put my hat on in a hurry.

4 알맞은 단어를 써서 대화를 완성하세요.

❶

A: The firefighters are p_____ _____ the fire.

B: I think they are very brave and strong.

❷

A: My students are always making noise.

B: How do you p_____ _____ _____ that?

❸

A: What a mess! Where is Oliver?

B: He saw you and r_____ _____.

---- 91 ----

run down
(기계, 건전지 등이) 멈추다, 다 되다
The battery has run down.
배터리가 떨어졌다.

run for
출마하다

run for election
선거에 출마하다

---

1 빈칸에 알맞은 구동사를 써보세요.

① 내 시계가 멈췄다.　　　　**My watch has** [____] [____] **.**

② 대통령에 출마하다　　　　[____] [____] **President**

2 빈칸에 알맞은 말을 써서 문장을 완성하세요.

① **If** [_____]**, people cannot use the machine.**

　 기계가 멈추면 사람들이 그 기계를 사용할 수 없다. (a machine)

② **You should** [_____]**.**

　 당신은 시장에 출마해야 한다. (mayor)

3 밑줄 친 부분을 우리말 뜻에 맞도록 고쳐보세요.

① **These batteries can be recharged when they <u>calm down</u>.**

　 이 배터리들은 닳으면 다시 충전할 수 있다.

② **Do you want to <u>long for</u> school president this year?**

　 너 올해 학생회장에 출마하고 싶니?

4 빈칸을 영어로 바꿔보세요.

① **A: What's wrong with your laptop?** 네 노트북에 무슨 문제 있어?

　 B: _____ but there's no power outlet. 배터리가 다 됐는데 콘센트가 없네.

② **A: _____ re-election next year.** 킹 의원은 내년에 재선에 출마할 거예요.

　 B: Good, I will be voting for her then. 좋아요, 저는 그럼 그녀한테 투표할 거예요.

58

run into
우연히 만나다

run into your favorite singer
좋아하는 가수를 우연히 만나다

run out of
~을 다 써버리다

run out of gas
연료가 고갈되다

---

1 빈칸에 알맞은 구동사를 써보세요.

① 심각한 어려움에 직면하다 ☐☐☐☐ ☐☐☐☐ serious difficulties

② 우유가 떨어지다 ☐☐☐☐ ☐☐☐☐ ☐☐☐☐ milk

2 빈칸에 알맞은 말을 써서 문장을 완성하세요.

① **She** _____.

그녀는 버스 터미널에서 크리스와 우연이 마주쳤다. (the bus terminal)

② **They** _____.

그들은 아이디어가 떨어졌다. (ideas)

3 밑줄 친 부분을 우리말 뜻에 맞도록 고쳐보세요.

① **We looked into some trouble yesterday.**

우리는 어제 약간의 곤경에 처했다.

② **The grocery store has gotten out of bananas.**

그 식료품점은 바나나가 다 떨어졌다.

4 빈칸을 영어로 바꿔보세요.

① **A: Where did you meet each other?** 너희 둘 어디서 만났어?

B: _____ while I was walking on Apple Street.

내가 애플 스트리트를 걷고 있을 때 제니와 우연히 만났어.

② **A: What's wrong with the car?** 차에 뭔가 문제가 있어?

B: Nothing. It just _____. 아무 일도 아니야. 그냥 기름이 떨어졌어.

see off
배웅하다

see off my son
아들을 배웅하다

send for
~를 부르러
사람을 보내다

send for a vet
수의사를 부르러 보내다

VET

---

1 빈칸에 알맞은 구동사를 써보세요.

① 병사들을 최전방까지 배웅하다 ⬚⬚⬚ ⬚⬚⬚ soldiers to the front line

② 즉시 의사를 부르러 보내다 ⬚⬚⬚ ⬚⬚⬚ a doctor immediately

2 빈칸에 알맞은 말을 써서 문장을 완성하세요.

① **Thank you for** ⬚⬚⬚⬚⬚ .

저를 배웅하러 이렇게 멀리까지 와주셔서 감사합니다. (coming all the way)

② **Please** ⬚⬚⬚⬚⬚ **right away.**

경찰을 즉시 불러 주세요. (a police officer)

3 밑줄 친 부분을 우리말 뜻에 맞도록 고쳐보세요.

① **My parents picked me up at the airport.**

우리 부모님은 공항에서 저를 배웅해 주셨어요.

② **She sent her assistant with the sales figures for March.**

그녀는 3월 판매수치를 가지러 비서를 보냈어요.

4 빈칸을 영어로 바꿔보세요.

① **A: What are you doing this afternoon?** 오늘 오후에 뭐 할 거야?

B: I'm _____**at the train station.** 기차역에서 우리 오빠를 배웅할 거야.

② **A: My father's fallen down the stairs and hurt himself!** 우리 아빠가 계단에서 넘어져서 다치셨어요!

B: Quick, _____**!** 어서요, 구급차를 불러주세요!

60

set out
출발하다

set out on a long walk
긴 걷기를 출발하다

set up
설치하다, 세우다, 놓다

set up the computer
컴퓨터를 설치하다

---

1 빈칸에 알맞은 구동사를 써보세요.

① 음식을 사러 출발하다 ⬜ ⬜ to buy food

② 장비를 설치하다 ⬜ ⬜ the equipment

2 빈칸에 알맞은 말을 써서 문장을 완성하세요.

① **They** ⬜ **this morning.**
그들은 오늘 아침에 여행을 출발했다. (on their trip)

② **She** ⬜ **.**
그녀는 스스로 텐트를 설치했다. (by herself)

3 밑줄 친 부분을 우리말 뜻에 맞도록 고쳐보세요.

① **She took out on a long journey to return home.**
그녀는 집에 돌아가기 위해서 긴 여정을 출발했다.

② **The police took up blockades on the highway.**
경찰은 고속도로에 봉쇄선을 설치했다.

4 빈칸을 영어로 바꿔보세요.

① **A: Fantastic! The rain stopped _____!** 잘됐어! 우리가 출발하기 전에 비가 멈췄어!

   B: Great! It's going to be the best trip for us! 좋아! 우리에게 최고의 여행이 될 거야!

② **A: Wow, look at your window!** 우와, 창문 좀 봐!

   B: My dad _____ for me last month.
   우리 아빠가 지난달에 나를 위해 망원경을 설치하셨어.

1 그림에 알맞은 표현을 고르세요.

❶

set out ☐
see off ☐

❷

run down ☐
run for ☐

❸

run into ☐
set up ☐

❹

run out of ☐
send for ☐

2 우리말에 알맞게 단어를 배열하여 문장을 완성하세요.

❶ 그는 어제 여행을 출발했다.

on • out • set

He _____ _____ _____ his trip yesterday.

❷ 그들은 아이디어가 떨어졌다.

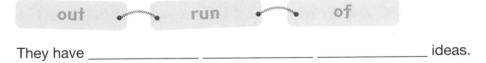

out • run • of

They have _____ _____ _____ ideas.

❸ 저를 배웅하러 이렇게 멀리까지 와주셔서 감사합니다.

me • see • off

Thank you for coming all the way to _____ _____ _____.

❹ 기계가 멈추면 사람들이 그 기계를 사용할 수 없다.

runs • a machine • down

If _____ _____ _____, people cannot use the machine.

3 그림을 보고 알맞은 문장과 연결하세요.

❶

❷

❸

❹

The battery has run down.

My parents saw me off at the airport.

My brother set up the computer for me.

We are going to run out of gas.

4 알맞은 단어를 써서 대화를 완성하세요.

❶

A: What's wrong with your mobile phone?

B: The battery has r_____ _____.

❷

A: Where did you meet Noah?

B: I r_____ _____ him when I went by Sunrise Park.

❸

A: Help, help! Someone has fallen down the stairs.

B: Please, s_____ _____ an ambulance!

61

settle into
적응하다

settle into a
new school
새 학교에 적응하다

show off
자랑하다

show off a new hat
새 모자를 자랑하다

---

1 빈칸에 알맞은 구동사를 써보세요.

① 새 집에 적응하다 　　　　　　　　　　　a new house

② 그녀의 능력들을 자랑하다 　　　　　　　　her abilities

2 빈칸에 알맞은 말을 써서 문장을 완성하세요.

① **They need time to** 　　　　　　　　　　　　.

그들은 대도시에 적응하는 데 시간이 필요하다. (the big city)

② **Some people take pictures to** 　　　　　　　　　　　　.

어떤 사람들은 그들의 상품들을 자랑하기 위해서 사진을 찍는다. (their products)

3 밑줄 친 부분을 우리말 뜻에 맞도록 고쳐보세요.

① **We provide information to help them <u>get into</u> their jobs.**

우리는 그들이 일에 적응하는 것을 돕기 위해 정보를 제공한다.

② **They started <u>getting off</u> their language skills.**

그들은 자신들의 언어 능력을 자랑하기 시작했다.

4 빈칸을 영어로 바꿔보세요.

① **A:** ＿＿＿＿＿＿＿＿＿＿＿＿＿＿＿＿＿**?** 당신 아이들은 새 학교에 적응을 어떻게 하고 있어요?

B: They are enjoying making new friends. 그들은 새 친구들을 사귀는 걸 즐기고 있어요.

② **A: Why did Jimmy want to see you?** 지미가 너를 왜 보고 싶어했어?

B: ＿＿＿＿＿＿＿＿＿＿＿＿＿＿＿＿**.**

그는 자신의 새 스마트 시계를 자랑하고 싶어했어.

show up
나타나다

show up in my dreams
내 꿈에 나타나다

sleep in
늦잠 자다

sleep in on Sundays
일요일마다 늦잠 자다

1 빈칸에 알맞은 구동사를 써보세요.

① 화면에 나타나다 ☐ ☐ **on the screen**

② 주말마다 늦잠 자다 ☐ ☐ **every weekend**

2 빈칸에 알맞은 말을 써서 문장을 완성하세요.

① **He** ☐ **.**

그는 한 시간 늦게 나타났다. (an hour later)

② **Jacob** ☐ **, so he was late for school.**

제이콥은 또 늦잠을 자서, 학교에 지각했다. (again)

3 밑줄 친 부분을 우리말 뜻에 맞도록 고쳐보세요.

① **He finally hanged up on the stage.**

그가 마침내 무대에 나타났다.

② **I'll stay up late tonight, so I'll check in tomorrow.**

나는 오늘 밤 늦게까지 안 잘 거라서 내일 늦잠 잘 거야.

4 빈칸을 영어로 바꿔보세요.

① **A: Are Jim and Dale expected to arrive soon?** 짐과 데일은 곧 도착할 예정이야?

B: Yes, but I'll be surprised _____. 응, 하지만 그들이 정각에 나타난다면 놀랄 일이지.

② **A: What did you do yesterday morning?** 어제 아침에 뭐 했어?

B: Not much. _____. 별거 안 했어. 오전 11시까지 늦잠 잤어.

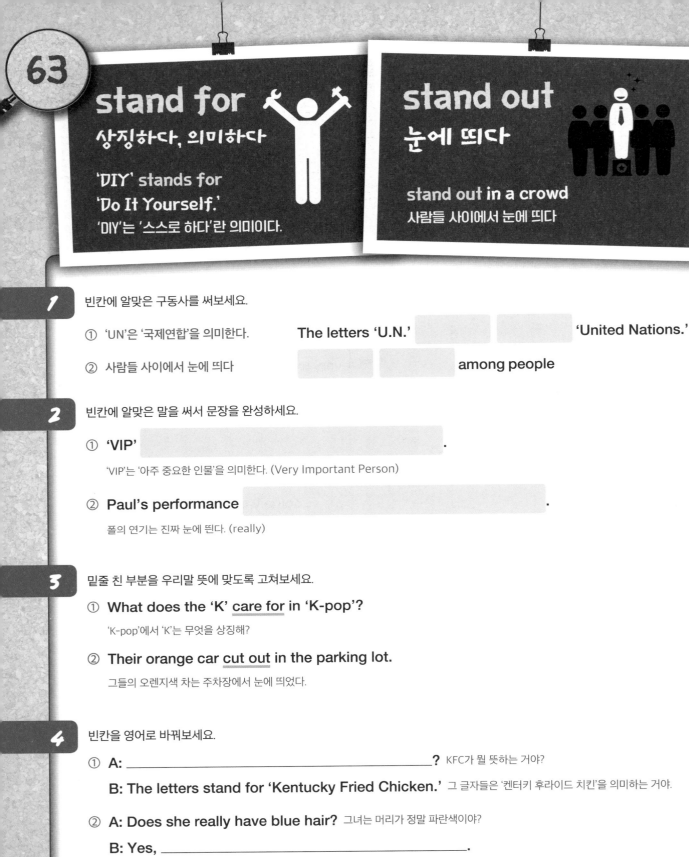

63

stand for
상징하다, 의미하다

'DIY' stands for
'Do It Yourself.'
'DIY'는 '스스로 하다'란 의미이다.

stand out
눈에 띄다

stand out in a crowd
사람들 사이에서 눈에 띄다

---

1 빈칸에 알맞은 구동사를 써보세요.

① 'UN'은 '국제연합'을 의미한다.　　The letters 'U.N.' _____ _____ 'United Nations.'

② 사람들 사이에서 눈에 띄다　　_____ _____ among people

2 빈칸에 알맞은 말을 써서 문장을 완성하세요.

① **'VIP'** _____.

　'VIP'는 '아주 중요한 인물'을 의미한다. (Very Important Person)

② **Paul's performance** _____.

　폴의 연기는 진짜 눈에 띈다. (really)

3 밑줄 친 부분을 우리말 뜻에 맞도록 고쳐보세요.

① **What does the 'K' <u>care for</u> in 'K-pop'?**

　'K-pop'에서 'K'는 무엇을 상징해?

② **Their orange car <u>cut out</u> in the parking lot.**

　그들의 오렌지색 차는 주차장에서 눈에 띄었다.

4 빈칸을 영어로 바꿔보세요.

① **A:** _____? KFC가 뭘 뜻하는 거야?

　B: The letters stand for 'Kentucky Fried Chicken.' 그 글자들은 '켄터키 후라이드 치킨'을 의미하는 거야.

② **A: Does she really have blue hair?** 그녀는 머리가 정말 파란색이야?

　B: Yes, _____.

　응, 그녀는 사람들 사이에서 눈에 띄어.

64

stand up for

~을 지지하다, 옹호하다

stand up for yourself
너 자신을 지지하다

stay up late

자지 않고 깨어 있다

stay up late at night
밤에 늦게까지 자지 않고
깨어 있다

---

1 빈칸에 알맞은 구동사를 써보세요.

① 당신의 권리를 옹호하다 _____ _____ _____ your rights

② 늦게까지 자지 않곤 했다 used to _____ _____ _____

2 빈칸에 알맞은 말을 써서 문장을 완성하세요.

① He _____ on his team.

그는 그의 팀의 모든 사람을 옹호했다. (everyone)

② Did you _____ ?

어젯밤에 늦게까지 자지 않은 거야? (last night)

3 밑줄 친 부분을 우리말 뜻에 맞도록 고쳐보세요.

① Why didn't you <u>stand for</u> me at the meeting?

너는 왜 회의 때 나를 지지하지 않은 거야?

② He wants to <u>put up with</u> to watch his favorite TV shows.

그는 자기가 좋아하는 TV쇼를 보려고 늦게까지 자지 않으려고 한다.

4 빈칸을 영어로 바꿔보세요.

① A: What do you like about your new team leader? 너희 새 팀장님 어떤 점이 좋은데?

   B: _____. 그녀는 항상 우리를 지지해줘.

② A: Why are you looking so tired? 너 왜 그렇게 피곤해 보여?

   B: _____. 어젯밤에 아주 늦게까지 깨어 있었어.

1 그림에 알맞은 표현을 고르세요.

❶

settle into ☐

stay up late ☐

❷

show up ☐

stand out ☐

❸

sleep in ☐

show off ☐

❹

stand for ☐

stand up for ☐

2 우리말에 알맞게 단어를 배열하여 문장을 완성하세요.

❶ 제이콥은 또 늦잠을 자서 학교에 지각했다.

> again ～ slept ～ in

Jacob _____ _____ _____, so he was late for school.

❷ 그들은 자신들의 언어 능력을 자랑하기 시작했다.

> off ～ showing ～ started

They _____ _____ _____ their language skills.

❸ 'VIP'는 '아주 중요한 인물'을 의미한다.

> stands ～ 'VIP' ～ for

_____ _____ _____ 'Very Important Person.'

❹ 그녀는 항상 우리를 지지해줘.

> stands ～ for ～ up

She always _____ _____ _____ us.

3 그림을 보고 알맞은 문장과 연결하세요.

①   •   • He finally showed up on the stage.

②   •   • He wants to show off a new hat.

③   •   • 'DIY' stands for 'Do It Yourself'.

④   •   • Did you stay up late last night?

4 알맞은 단어를 써서 대화를 완성하세요.

①

A: How are your pets s_____ _____ the new house?

B: They like it now.

②

A: What did you do this morning?

B: Not much. I s_____ _____ until 12:00.

③

A: Does she really have blue hair?

B: Yes, she s_____ _____ among people.

stretch out
뻗다

stretch out your
right hand
당신의 오른손을 뻗다

switch off
신경을 끄다

Please switch off.
제발 신경을 꺼주세요.

1 빈칸에 알맞은 구동사를 써보세요.

① 그의 긴 다리를 뻗다 _____ _____ his long legs

② 그냥 신경 좀 꺼줄래요? Would you just _____ _____ ?

2 빈칸에 알맞은 말을 써서 문장을 완성하세요.

① _____ and breathe in fresh air.

팔을 쭉 뻗고 신선한 공기를 들이마셔요. (your arms)

② I _____ he starts talking about cars.

그가 차에 대해 말하기 시작하면 나는 신경을 꺼요. (when)

3 밑줄 친 부분을 우리말 뜻에 맞도록 고쳐보세요.

① The baby <u>pointed out</u> his hand to grab his mom.

그 아기는 엄마를 붙잡기 위해 손을 뻗었다.

② If you don't care about animation, <u>see off</u> now.

만화 영화에 관심이 없으면 이제부터 신경을 끄세요.

4 빈칸을 영어로 바꿔보세요.

① A: Could you move your seat forward? _____.

좌석을 앞으로 움직여주실래요? 제가 다리를 뻗을 수가 없어서요.

B: Oh, I'll move forward. 오, 제가 앞으로 갈게요.

② A: Is the principal a good speaker? 교장 선생님은 연설 잘하시니?

B: Not really. _____ as soon as he starts speaking.

별로. 학생들은 교장 선생님이 말하기 시작하자마자 신경을 꺼버리지.

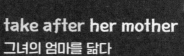

take after
닮다

take after her mother
그녀의 엄마를 닮다

take apart
분해하다

take apart the engine
엔진을 분해하다

1 빈칸에 알맞은 구동사를 써보세요.

① 우리 이모를 닮다 ⬚⬚⬚ ⬚⬚⬚ **my aunt**

② TV를 분해하다 ⬚⬚⬚ ⬚⬚⬚ **a TV**

2 빈칸에 알맞은 말을 써서 문장을 완성하세요.

① **The girl** ⬚⬚⬚⬚⬚⬚⬚⬚⬚⬚**.**

그 소녀는 자기 할머니를 닮았다. (her grandmother)

② **I** ⬚⬚⬚⬚⬚⬚⬚⬚⬚⬚ **to fix it.**

나는 컴퓨터를 고치기 위해 분해했다. (the computer)

3 밑줄 친 부분을 우리말 뜻에 맞도록 고쳐보세요.

① **People say I ask after my uncle.**

사람들은 내가 삼촌을 닮았다고 말한다.

② **Taking away the drone was easy.**

드론을 분해하는 것은 쉬웠다.

4 빈칸을 영어로 바꿔보세요.

① **A: Does your daughter look like you?** 네 딸은 너를 닮았어?

B: No, _____. 아니, 그녀는 자기 아빠를 닮았어.

② **A: What's wrong with your watch?** 네 시계 왜 그래?

B: It's broken, so _____. 시계가 고장 났어, 그래서 내가 그것을 분해했지.

take away
갖고 가다, 없애다
take away the boxes
상자들을 치우다

take back
(자기가 한 말을) 취소하다
take back my words
내 말을 취소하다

1 빈칸에 알맞은 구동사를 써보세요.

① 스트레스를 없애다 [   ] [   ] the stress

② 내가 한 말을 취소하다 [   ] [   ] what I said

2 빈칸에 알맞은 말을 써서 문장을 완성하세요.

① **Please** [   ].

더러운 접시들은 치워주세요. (the dirty dishes)

② **I am sorry. I** [   ].

미안해. 내 말을 취소할게. (my words)

3 밑줄 친 부분을 우리말 뜻에 맞도록 고쳐보세요.

① **People say that time will <u>run away</u> the pain.**

사람들은 시간이 고통을 없애줄 거라고 말한다.

② **You can't <u>call back</u> what you said on TV.**

당신은 당신이 TV에서 한 말을 취소할 수 없다.

4 빈칸을 영어로 바꿔보세요.

① **A: Why were the students in Ms. Bennet's class so unhappy?**

베넷 씨 반 학생들은 왜 기분이 안 좋았던 거야?

B: Because _____. 그녀가 그들의 휴대전화를 모두 빼앗아서 그래.

② **A: I think** _____ **about Don!** 네가 돈에 대해 한 말은 취소해야 할 거 같아!

B: Alright. He's not ugly. He's kind of cute. 그래. 그는 못생기지 않았어. 좀 귀여워.

take off
이륙하다

The plane took off a few minutes ago.
비행기는 몇 분 전에 이륙했다.

take out
꺼내다, 빼내다

take out a book from the bookshelf
책장에서 책을 한 권 꺼내다

1 빈칸에 알맞은 구동사를 써보세요.

① 비행기들이 이륙하려고 대기중이다.   The planes are waiting to _____ _____.

② 그녀의 지갑에서 돈을 조금 꺼내다   _____ _____ some money from her wallet

2 빈칸에 알맞은 말을 써서 문장을 완성하세요.

① **Three planes are** _____.

　　세 대의 비행기가 동시에 이륙하고 있어요. (at the same time)

② **You may need to have a tooth** _____.

　　너는 오늘 이빨 한 개를 뽑아야 할지 몰라. (today)

3 밑줄 친 부분을 우리말 뜻에 맞도록 고쳐보세요.

① **I saw the plane getting off at the airport.**

　　나는 공항에서 비행기가 이륙하는 걸 봤다.

② **William found out some candies from the box.**

　　윌리엄은 상자에서 사탕을 몇 개 꺼냈다.

4 빈칸을 영어로 바꿔보세요.

① **A: Can I use the restroom?** 화장실을 사용해도 될까요?

　 B: Sorry, you can't. The plane will _____.

　　죄송하지만, 안됩니다. 비행기가 약 2분 후에 이륙할 예정이라서요.

② **A:** _____ **from the overhead bin?**

　　머리 위 짐칸에서 여행 가방을 꺼내주시겠어요?

　 B: No problem! I'll help you. 그럼요! 제가 도와드릴게요.

1 그림에 알맞은 표현을 고르세요.

①

stretch out ☐

take away ☐

②

take off ☐

switch off ☐

③

take out ☐

take apart ☐

④

take after ☐

take back ☐

2 우리말에 알맞게 단어를 배열하여 문장을 완성하세요.

① 미안해, 내 말을 취소할게.

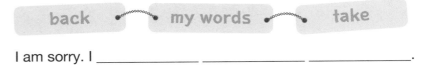

back • my words • take

I am sorry. I _____ _____ _____.

② 사람들은 내가 삼촌을 닮았다고 말한다.

after • take • my uncle

People say I _____ _____ _____.

③ 스포츠에 관심이 없으면 이제부터 신경을 끄세요.

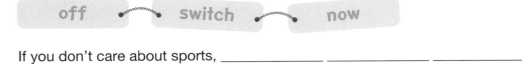

off • switch • now

If you don't care about sports, _____ _____ _____.

④ 그는 상자에서 초콜릿을 몇 개 꺼냈다.

took • some chocolate • out

He _____ _____ _____ from the box.

3 그림을 보고 알맞은 문장과 연결하세요.

❶

❷

❸

❹

He took a book out from the bookshelf.

Please take away the dirty dishes.

Susan takes after her mother.

Would you just switch off, please?

4 알맞은 단어를 써서 대화를 완성하세요.

❶

A: I'm so nervous. What can I do?

B: S_____ _____ your arms and count to 10.

❷

A: What happened to the computer?

B: It's not working, so I t_____ it _____.

❸

A: Oh, I can't t_____ _____ the suitcase from the overhead bin.

B: Don't worry. I'll help you.

take over
넘겨받다, 물려받다
take over the work
일을 넘겨받다

take up ①
(시간, 장소를) 차지하다
take up a lot of time
시간을 많이 뺏다

1 빈칸에 알맞은 구동사를 써보세요.

① 그녀의 업무를 넘겨받다 　　　　　　　　　 her duties

② 자리를 너무 많이 차지하다 　　　　　　　　　 too much room

2 빈칸에 알맞은 말을 써서 문장을 완성하세요.

① I will 　　　　　　　　　　　　 for a week.

제가 일주일 동안 에이미의 일을 대신 맡을 거예요. (Amy's job)

② It won't 　　　　　　　　　　　.

당신 시간을 많이 뺏지는 않을 거예요. (much of your time)

3 밑줄 친 부분을 우리말 뜻에 맞도록 고쳐보세요.

① She got over the business from her grandfather.

그녀는 할아버지 사업을 물려받았다.

② These files hold up a lot of space on your computer.

이 파일들은 당신 컴퓨터의 공간을 많이 차지한다.

4 빈칸을 영어로 바꿔보세요.

① A: When did you start working here? 당신은 언제 여기서 일하기 시작했어요?

B: ＿＿＿＿＿＿＿＿＿＿ from Jarvis last month. 지난달에 자비스한테 일을 인수인계 받았어요.

② A: Did you finish the report that I asked for? 제가 요청한 보고서 끝냈나요?

B: Sorry, the team meeting ＿＿＿＿＿＿＿＿＿.

죄송합니다, 팀 회의에 아침 시간을 거의 다 뺏겼어요.

tell apart
구별하다

tell apart the twins
쌍둥이를 구별하다

think over
심사숙고하다

think over
the proposal
그 제안을 심사숙고하다

---

1 빈칸에 알맞은 구동사를 써보세요.

① 서로 다른 아시아 국가들의 사람들을 구별하다 ⬜ different Asian races ⬜

② 그녀의 말을 심사숙고하다 ⬜ ⬜ her words

2 빈칸에 알맞은 말을 써서 문장을 완성하세요.

① **They look alike, so I** ⬜.

그들은 서로 닮아서 나는 그들을 구별할 수 없다. (can't)

② **Please** ⬜ **very carefully.**

당신 입장을 아주 신중하게 심사숙고해 주세요. (your position)

3 밑줄 친 부분을 우리말 뜻에 맞도록 고쳐보세요.

① **Can dogs <u>take apart</u> different colors?**

개들은 서로 다른 색깔을 구별할 수 있나요?

② **We should <u>get over</u> all the options.**

우리는 모든 선택사항들을 고려해야 해요.

4 빈칸을 영어로 바꿔보세요.

① **A: The tastes of these two soups are very similar.** 이 두 개의 수프 맛이 매우 비슷해.

B: Yes, _____. 맞아, 난 구별 못 하겠어.

② **A: _____ before you answer.**

대답하기 전에 그 제안을 아주 주의 깊게 고려하세요.

B: OK. I plan to. 알겠어요. 저도 그러려고 해요.

---- 111 ----

throw away
버리다

throw away old shoes
낡은 신발을 버리다

throw up
토하다

throw up in the sink
싱크대에 토하다

---

1 빈칸에 알맞은 구동사를 써보세요.

① 남은 음식을 버리다 　　　　　　　　　　　 the leftovers

② 화장실에 가서 토하다 　go to the toilet and 　　　　　　

2 빈칸에 알맞은 말을 써서 문장을 완성하세요.

① **You should** 　　　　　　　　　　　　　　　　.

　　당신은 그것을 쓰레기통에 버려야 한다. (in the garbage bin)

② **I feel like** 　　　　　　　　　　　　　.

　　나 토할 것 같아. (be going to)

3 밑줄 친 부분을 우리말 뜻에 맞도록 고쳐보세요.

① **Should I <u>get away</u> these old books?**

　　이 헌책들을 버려야 할까?

② **If you are going to <u>grow up</u>, tell me first.**

　　토할 것 같으면 나한테 먼저 말해.

4 빈칸을 영어로 바꿔보세요.

① **A: I don't want to** ＿＿＿＿＿＿＿＿＿＿＿＿＿＿＿. 난 이 낡은 의자를 버리고 싶지 않아.

　　B: Then you should keep it in your room. 그러면 그것을 네 방에 두어야 돼.

② **A: You don't look well.** 너 안 좋아 보여.

　　B: I feel sick. ＿＿＿＿＿＿＿＿＿＿＿＿＿＿ **in the toilet.**

　　　나 속이 안 좋아. 화장실에 가서 토할래.

tie up
묶다

tie up your shoelaces
신발끈을 묶다

try on
입어보다

try on a pair of jeans
청바지 한 벌을 입어보다

1 빈칸에 알맞은 구동사를 써보세요.

① 풍선을 묶다 ⬚ ⬚ the balloon

② 갈색 코트를 입어보다 ⬚ ⬚ the brown coat

2 빈칸에 알맞은 말을 써서 문장을 완성하세요.

① **She** _____ **every morning.**

그녀는 매일 아침 머리를 묶는다. (her hair)

② **Let me** _____.

빨간색 블라우스를 입어볼게요. (the red blouse)

3 밑줄 친 부분을 우리말 뜻에 맞도록 고쳐보세요.

① **She didn't line up the horse in the barn yesterday.**

그녀는 어제 헛간에 말을 묶어 두지 않았다.

② **I put several outfits up, but nothing seemed right.**

나는 옷을 몇 벌 입어봤지만 알맞아 보이는 게 없었다.

4 빈칸을 영어로 바꿔보세요.

① **A:** _____ **before we give it to Dad?** 아빠한테 드리기 전에 선물을 묶어야 할까?

B: Yes. Add a bow on top. 그래. 위에 나비 모양 리본을 달아.

② **A: Good afternoon. What can I help you with?** 좋은 오후입니다. 무엇을 도와드릴까요?

B: _____**?** 그 재킷을 입어볼 수 있을까요?

Review

1 그림에 알맞은 표현을 고르세요.

❶

throw up ☐

throw away ☐

❷

take up ☐

tell apart ☐

❸

tie up ☐

try on ☐

❹

take over ☐

think over ☐

2 우리말에 알맞게 단어를 배열하여 문장을 완성하세요.

❶ 당신은 각각의 개들을 구분할 수 있나요?

Can you _____ _____ _____ from one another?

❷ 그는 그의 할아버지의 사업을 물려받았다.

He _____ _____ _____ from his grandfather.

❸ 그녀는 매일 아침에 그녀의 머리를 묶는다.

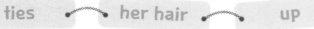

She _____ _____ _____ every morning.

❹ 나 토할 것 같아.

I feel like I'm going _____ _____ _____.

3 그림을 보고 알맞은 문장과 연결하세요.

①   •

②   •

③   •

④   •

• The twins look alike, so I can't tell them apart.

• I will take over the work for a week.

• Tie up your shoelaces, or you will fall.

• I think I am going to throw up.

4 알맞은 단어를 써서 대화를 완성하세요.

①

A: Can you t_____ the two flags _____?

B: No, I can't. They are very similar.

②

A: Should I t_____ _____ these old books?

B: Yes. I think they took up too much room.

③

A: Can I t_____ _____ these jeans?

B: Sure. The fitting room is over there.

try out
시험 삼아 해보다

try out a new video game
새 비디오 게임을 해보다

turn around
돌다, 돌아서다

turn around at the end of the road
길 끝에서 돌다

1 빈칸에 알맞은 구동사를 써보세요.

① 새 스케이트보드를 타보다 ⬜ ⬜ a new skateboard

② 나를 보려고 돌아서다 ⬜ ⬜ to see me

2 빈칸에 알맞은 말을 써서 문장을 완성하세요.

① **Would you like to** ⬜ ?

전기 자동차 타보고 싶어? (an electric car)

② **He** ⬜ .

그는 돌아서서 도망쳤다. (run away)

3 밑줄 친 부분을 우리말 뜻에 맞도록 고쳐보세요.

① **Have you <u>set out</u> your new computer yet?**

새 컴퓨터를 벌써 시험해봤어?

② **<u>Get around</u> and go back to your seat.**

돌아서서 자리로 돌아가세요.

4 빈칸을 영어로 바꿔보세요.

① **A: What are you doing?** 너 뭐 하고 있어?

　B: _____ **before the game.** 경기 전에 새 운동화를 신어보려고 하고 있어.

② **A: Did you see my phone?** 내 전화기 봤어?

　B: _____ **and you'll find it.** 돌아봐, 그러면 그것을 찾을 수 있을 거야.

turn down
거절하다

turn down a proposal
제안을 거절하다

turn into
~으로 변하다

turn into a butterfly
나비로 변하다

---

1 빈칸에 알맞은 구동사를 써보세요.

① 일자리를 거절하다   [ ]   [ ]   a job offer

② 착한 학생이 되다   [ ]   [ ]   a good student

2 빈칸에 알맞은 말을 써서 문장을 완성하세요.

① **Why did you** _____?

엠마의 초대를 왜 거절했어? (Emma's invitation)

② **Do you know** _____?

어떻게 우유가 치즈로 변하는지 알아? (cheese)

3 밑줄 친 부분을 우리말 뜻에 맞도록 고쳐보세요.

① **Her idea was <u>handed down</u> by them.**

그녀의 아이디어는 그들에게 거절당했다.

② **How do good people <u>look into</u> bad people?**

착한 사람들이 어떻게 나쁜 사람들로 변해?

4 빈칸을 영어로 바꿔보세요.

① **A: This laptop is only $80 if you want it.** 원하시면 이 노트북을 단 80달러에 드릴게요.

    B: That's a steal! _____?

공짜나 다름없네요! 제가 어떻게 그것을 거절할 수 있겠어요?

② **A: Why does he like the new robot?** 그는 왜 그 새 로봇을 좋아해?

    B: Because his new robot _____.

그의 새 로봇은 차로 변할 수 있기 때문이야.

turn off
(전기, 가스 등을) 끄다

turn off the TV
TV를 끄다

turn on
(전기, 가스 등을) 켜다

turn on the heater
히터를 켜다

1 빈칸에 알맞은 구동사를 써보세요.

① 불을 끄다 　　　　　　　　　　　　　the light

② 에어컨을 켜다 　　　　　　　　　　　　the air conditioner

2 빈칸에 알맞은 말을 써서 문장을 완성하세요.

① I 　　　　　　　　　　　　　　　　 after I get up.

나는 일어난 다음 알람 시계를 끈다. (the alarm clock)

② **Can you tell me how to** 　　　　　　　　　　　　　　 **?**

이 휴대전화 켜는 법 좀 알려줄래? (this cell phone)

3 밑줄 친 부분을 우리말 뜻에 맞도록 고쳐보세요.

① **Don't forget to put off the gas before you go out.**

외출하기 전에 가스불 끄는 거 잊지 마.

② **Try on the music, please.**

음악 좀 틀어주세요.

4 빈칸을 영어로 바꿔보세요.

① **A: Is it okay to** _____**?** 컴퓨터를 지금 꺼도 괜찮아?

B: I think so. It's finished updating the programs. 그럴 거 같아. 프로그램 업데이트가 끝났어.

② **A: I can't see anything.** 아무것도 안 보여.

B: You need to _____**.** 네가 불을 켜야 할 것 같아.

turn out
~로 판명되다

turn out to be true
진실로 판명되다

turn over
뒤집다

The baby can turn over.
아기가 뒤집을 수 있다.

---

1 빈칸에 알맞은 구동사를 써보세요.

① 근거가 없는 것으로 판명되다 　　　　　　　　　**to be groundless**

② 게들은 스스로 뒤집는다. 　　**The crabs** 　　　　　　 **by themselves.**

2 빈칸에 알맞은 말을 써서 문장을 완성하세요.

① **I'm glad that things** 　　　　　　　　　　　　 **in the end.**

결국 모든 게 잘 돼서 기쁘다. (well)

② **The truck** 　　　　　　　　　　　 **the driver.**

트럭이 뒤집혀서 운전사가 부상을 입었다. (injure)

3 밑줄 친 부분을 우리말 뜻에 맞도록 고쳐보세요.

① **The rumor <u>took out</u> to be false.**

그 소문은 거짓으로 판명되었다.

② **The ship <u>took over</u> and sank too fast.**

그 배는 뒤집혀서 너무 빨리 가라앉았다.

4 빈칸을 영어로 바꿔보세요.

① **A: I really don't know if we can finish on time.** 우리가 제 시간에 마칠 수 있을지 정말 모르겠어.

　B: Don't worry. ＿＿＿＿＿＿＿＿＿＿＿＿＿＿＿. 걱정하지 마. 모든 게 다 잘될 거야.

② **A: The doctor will** ＿＿＿＿＿＿＿＿＿＿＿ **onto your back.**

　　의사가 당신에게 돌아서 등을 대고 누우라고 할 거예요.

　B: Okay. Until she does, can I lie on my front? 그녀가 말할 때까지 앞으로 누워 있어도 될까요?

1 그림에 알맞은 표현을 고르세요.

①

turn on ☐

turn down ☐

②

turn out ☐

try out ☐

③

turn into ☐

turn off ☐

④

turn over ☐

turn around ☐

2 우리말에 알맞게 단어를 배열하여 문장을 완성하세요.

① 그는 돌아서서 도망쳤다.

turned ⌇ He ⌇ around

_____ _____ _____ and ran away.

② 심심해요. 음악을 틀어주세요.

the music ⌇ on ⌇ Turn

I'm bored. _____ _____ _____, please.

③ 왜 그녀의 초대를 거절했어?

down ⌇ turn ⌇ you

Why did _____ _____ _____ her invitation?

④ 결국 모든 게 잘돼서 기뻐.

well ⌇ turned ⌇ out

I'm glad that things _____ _____ _____ in the end.

3 그림을 보고 알맞은 문장과 연결하세요.

❶

•   • The rumor turned out to be true.

❷

•   • It's too cold. Can you turn on the heater?

❸

•   • Please turn around at the end of the road.

❹

•   • How does a caterpillar turn into a butterfly?

4 알맞은 단어를 써서 대화를 완성하세요.

❶

A: Would you like to t_____ _____ this new phone?

B: Fantastic! I love it.

❷

A: This hairband is only $1.

B: That's a steal. How can I t_____ that _____?

❸

A: Don't forget to t_____ _____ the computer before you leave.

B: Don't worry about it.

turn to
의지하다

turn to my older sister
우리 언니에게 의지하다

wait on
(식사)
시중을 들다

wait on the guest
손님을 시중들다

---

1 빈칸에 알맞은 구동사를 써보세요.

① 게임과 인터넷에 의지하다 _____ _____ games and the Internet

② 동시에 두 손님을 시중들다 _____ _____ two customers at once

2 빈칸에 알맞은 말을 써서 문장을 완성하세요.

① I always _____ .

나는 곤경에 빠졌을 때 항상 책에 의지한다. (in trouble)

② I am going to _____ today.

나는 오늘 그들을 시중들 예정이다. (them)

3 밑줄 친 부분을 우리말 뜻에 맞도록 고쳐보세요.

① Who does Paul <u>look to</u> when he feels sad?

폴은 슬플 때 누구한테 의지해?

② My mom is very sick, so I will <u>rely on</u> her all day.

엄마가 많이 아프셔서 나는 하루 종일 그녀를 시중들 거야.

4 빈칸을 영어로 바꿔보세요.

① A: You need to speak to someone else for help. 당신은 다른 누군가에게 도와달라고 말해야 해요.

B: No, _____. 아뇨, 당신이 제가 의지할 수 있는 유일한 사람이에요.

② A: Can you get me a sandwich? 나 샌드위치 하나 사다줄래?

B: _____. Get it yourself!

내가 너무 피곤해서 네 시중 못 들겠어. 네가 직접 사다 먹어!

watch out (for)
(~을) 조심하다

Hey, watch out!
이봐, 조심해!

wear out
닳다

wear out over time
시간이 지나면서 닳다

---

1 빈칸에 알맞은 구동사를 써보세요.

① 모두들 조심하세요!   ⬚⬚⬚⬚ ⬚⬚⬚⬚ , everyone!

② 브레이크가 닳다   brakes ⬚⬚⬚ ⬚⬚⬚

2 빈칸에 알맞은 말을 써서 문장을 완성하세요.

① **You will fall into the pool** ⬚⬚⬚⬚⬚⬚⬚⬚⬚⬚ !

당신 조심하지 않으면 웅덩이에 빠질 거예요. (if)

② **Why do my shoes** ⬚⬚⬚⬚⬚⬚⬚⬚ **on one side?**

내 신발은 왜 한쪽이 더 빠르게 닳을까? (faster)

3 밑줄 친 부분을 우리말 뜻에 맞도록 고쳐보세요.

① **You need to <u>put out</u> for rocks on the road.**

여러분은 도로 위 암석들을 조심해야 합니다.

② **The carpet on the stairs <u>picked out</u> and looked dirty.**

계단에 깔린 카펫이 닳아서 지저분해 보였다.

4 빈칸을 영어로 바꿔보세요.

① **A: Did the tour operator warn you about shopping at the market?**

여행 전문가가 시장에서 물건을 사는 것에 대해 주의를 줬나요?

B: We were told to _____. 가짜 보석을 조심하라고 들었어요.

② **A: What was the biggest benefit of using those tires?** 그 타이어를 사용하는 가장 큰 장점은 뭐였죠?

B: _____. 그것은 빨리 닳지 않았어요.

work out
운동하다

work out every day
매일 운동하다

wrap up
마무리를 짓다, 끝내다

wrap up the class
수업을 마무리 짓다

---

1 빈칸에 알맞은 구동사를 써보세요.

① 저녁에 운동하다 ☐☐☐☐☐ ☐☐☐☐☐ **in the evening**

② 프로젝트를 마무리 짓다 ☐☐☐☐☐ ☐☐☐☐☐ **the project**

---

2 빈칸에 알맞은 말을 써서 문장을 완성하세요.

① I ☐☐☐☐☐☐☐☐☐☐.

나는 일주일에 세 번 운동한다. (three times a week)

② It's time to ☐☐☐☐☐☐☐☐☐.

하시던 것을 마무리할 시간이에요. (what you are doing)

---

3 밑줄 친 부분을 우리말 뜻에 맞도록 고쳐보세요.

① **<u>Standing out</u> regularly is a good way to lose weight.**

규칙적으로 운동하는 것은 살을 빼는 좋은 방법이다.

② **Shall we <u>take up</u> the meeting now?**

지금 회의를 마무리 지을까요?

---

4 빈칸을 영어로 바꿔보세요.

① **A: How often do you exercise?** 너는 얼마나 자주 운동해?

B: _____. 난 매일 운동해.

② **A: When should I expect you to arrive?** 너 언제 도착할 예정이야?

B: I will _____ **by noon. So, shortly after that.**

낮 12시까지 일을 마무리할 거라서 그 직후에.

---

write down
적어 놓다

write down the recipe
요리법을 적어 놓다

zoom in
확대하다

zoom in on the actor's face
배우의 얼굴을 확대하다

1 빈칸에 알맞은 구동사를 써보세요.

① 중요한 점들을 적어 놓다 　　　　　　　　　　　　 important points

② 배경을 확대하다 　　　　　　　　　　　　 on the background

2 빈칸에 알맞은 말을 써서 문장을 완성하세요.

① I'll 　　　　　　　　　　　　 for her.

그녀를 위해 전화번호를 적어 놓을게. (the phone number)

② She 　　　　　　　　　　　　 on the map.

그녀는 지도에서 그 지하철역을 확대했다. (on the subway station)

3 밑줄 친 부분을 우리말 뜻에 맞도록 고쳐보세요.

① Could you <u>turn that down</u> on the whiteboard, please?

화이트 보드에 그것을 적어주실래요?

② You can <u>settle in</u> by double-clicking on the map.

지도에서 더블 클릭하면 확대할 수 있어요.

4 빈칸을 영어로 바꿔보세요.

① A: ＿＿＿＿＿＿＿＿＿＿＿＿＿＿＿ helps me to remember them better.

무언가 적어 두면 더 잘 기억하는 데 도움이 돼.

B: Me, too. Memorizing them doesn't always work. 나도. 그것들이 항상 외워지는 게 아니라서.

② A: It's hard to tell who it is. 그게 누구인지 알아보기 힘들어.

B: ＿＿＿＿＿＿＿＿＿＿＿＿＿＿＿ you can see the person's face better.

사진을 확대하면 그 사람 얼굴이 더 잘 보일 거야.

1 그림에 알맞은 표현을 고르세요.

 ❶

 ❷

 ❸

 ❹

wait on ☐   wear out ☐   write down ☐   wrap up ☐

watch out ☐   work out ☐   zoom in ☐   turn to ☐

2 우리말에 알맞게 단어를 배열하여 문장을 완성하세요.

❶ 조심하지 않으면 웅덩이에 빠질 거예요.

out   watch   don't

You will fall into the pool if you _____ _____ _____!

❷ 나는 일주일에 세 번 운동한다.

out   work   I

_____ _____ _____ three times a week.

❸ 그는 슬플 때 누구한테 의지해?

turn   he   to

Who does _____ _____ _____ when he feels sad?

❹ 나는 중요한 점들을 적어 놓을 것이다.

the important points   down   write

I'll _____ _____ _____.

그림을 보고 알맞은 문장과 연결하세요.

① • • I can't see it. Can you zoom in on his face?

② • • I turn to my older sister.

③ • • Hey, watch out! There are rocks on the road.

④ • • Working out every day is good for your health.

 알맞은 단어를 써서 대화를 완성하세요.

①
A: Oh, no! Look at the rug. It's w_____ _____.

B: Let's go shopping for a new one.

②
A: It's time to w_____ _____ what you are doing.

B: That was fun. Can we do it again tomorrow?

③
A: What can help me remember things better?

B: W_____ things _____ helps me remember them better.

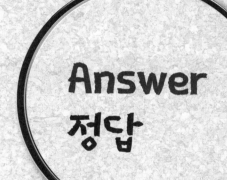
Answer
정답

Answer

01 ask after / ask for

1 ① ask after their health
　 ② ask for a menu

2 ① They asked after my grandfather.
　 ② The man asked for help in English.

3 ① asks with ➜ asks after
　 ② go for ➜ ask for

4 ① A: Did Jason ask after me?
　 ② B: It's too difficult. I should ask for help.

02 back up / be into

1 ① back up about two meters
　 ② be into fashion

2 ① Can you back up a few steps, please?
　 ② I am into science these days.

3 ① got up ➜ backed up
　 ② is over ➜ is into

4 ① B: Oh, I see! I have to back up a little.
　 ② B: I'm into history now.

03 be over / blow out

1 ① will be over after two
　 ② blow out all the candles

2 ① When will your class be over today?
　 ② Blow out the candles and make a wish.

3 ① be out ➜ be over
　 ② cut out ➜ blow out

4 ① B: Be patient. The movie will be over soon.
　 ② B: You should blow them out.

04 boot up / break down

1 ① boot up the laptop
　 ② break down again

2 ① I can't boot up my computer again.
　 ② My bike suddenly broke down.

3 ① back up ➜ boot up
　 ② took down ➜ broke down

4 ① B: I can't boot up my old computer again.
　 ② B: Sorry, I'll be late. My bike broke down again.

01 Review

1 ❶ blow out ❷ break down ❸ back up
　 ❹ ask for

2 ❶ They asked after my grandmother.
　 ❷ I am into science these days.
　 ❸ Be patient. The movie will be over soon.

❹ I will <u>boot up the beam projector[boot the beam projector up]</u>.

3 ❶ I can't boot up my computer again.
❷ When will your class be over today?
❸ Can you back up a few steps, please?
❹ The man asked for help in English.

4 ❶ A: <u>Blow out</u> the candles and make a wish.
❷ B: I a<u>m into</u> hip-hop music now.
❸ B: Sorry, I'll be late. My bike b<u>roke down</u> again.

05 break into / break out

1 ① <u>break into</u> his office
② A fight <u>broke out</u>.

2 ① A thief <u>broke into my house</u>.
② A big fire <u>broke out downtown</u>.

3 ① break out ➜ <u>break into</u>
② carried out ➜ <u>broke out</u>

4 ① B: <u>A thief broke into my house last night</u>.
② A: <u>A fire broke out downtown</u> during the night.

06 bring back / bring over

1 ① <u>bring back</u> the book
② <u>bring over</u> some sandwiches

2 ① When will you <u>bring back the tablet</u>?
② I will <u>bring Julian over today</u>.

3 ① bring down ➜ <u>bring back</u>
② taking over ➜ <u>bringing over</u>

4 ① B: <u>When will you bring it back</u>?
② B: Sure. And <u>I will bring Brad over tonight</u>.

07 bring up / burst into

1 ① <u>bring up</u> the idea
② <u>burst into</u> laughter

2 ① She <u>brought up the topic</u>.
② Why did they <u>burst into laughter</u>?

3 ① brought down ➜ <u>brought up</u>
② got into ➜ <u>burst into</u>

4 ① B: <u>Don't bring up that topic</u> with her. She gets very angry.
② A: <u>Why did she burst into tears</u>?

08 call back / call off

1 ① will <u>call</u> him <u>back</u> this afternoon
② <u>call off</u> the game

2 ① I <u>called back several times</u>.
② They <u>called off the baseball game</u>.

3 ① bring him back ➜ <u>call him back</u>
② got off ➜ <u>called off</u>

Answer

4 ① B: No, but <u>I'll call him back this afternoon</u>.

② B: <u>Are we calling off the soccer game</u> then?

1 ❶ break into ❷ bring back ❸ burst into ❹ call off

2 ❶ <u>A fight broke out</u> between two groups.
❷ Jake <u>is bringing over</u> his friend tonight.
❸ I'll <u>call him back</u> this afternoon.
❹ They <u>called off the game[called the game off]</u>.

3 ❶ He brought up the topic.
❷ I will bring him over tonight.
❸ A big fire broke out downtown.
❹ I called back several times.

4 ❶ A: Why did she b<u>urst into</u> tears?
❷ B: When will you b<u>ring</u> it <u>back</u>?
❸ B: I'm sorry. I'll c<u>all</u> you <u>back</u> this afternoon.

1 ① <u>call</u> <u>out</u> very loudly to him
② <u>call</u> her <u>up</u>

2 ① Jamie <u>called out to his mother for help</u>.
② I'll <u>call them up this week</u>.

3 ① called back ➜ <u>called out</u>
② call her off ➜ <u>call her up</u>

4 ① A: <u>Did you call out for help</u>?
② B: No, but <u>I'll call them up this weekend</u>.

1 ① <u>care</u> <u>about</u> other people's feelings
② <u>care</u> <u>for</u> elderly patients

2 ① I really <u>care about you a lot</u>.
② Vets <u>care for sick pets</u>.

3 ① worry about ➜ <u>care about</u>
② looking for ➜ <u>caring for</u>

4 ① B: Yeah. <u>She doesn't care about anyone</u> but herself.
② A: <u>Who will care for the patients</u>?

1 ① <u>calm</u> <u>down</u> for a second
② <u>carry</u> <u>out</u> a survey

2 ① <u>Calm down a bit</u> and breathe!
② We have to <u>carry out the mission</u>.

3 ① Hand down ➜ <u>Calm down</u>
② point out ➜ <u>carry out</u>

4 ① A: I think <u>you need to calm down</u>.
② B: You should <u>carry out the plan right</u>

12 cheat on / check in

1 ① <u>cheat on</u> an exam
② <u>check in</u> for the flight

2 ① Why did you <u>cheat on the test</u>?
② I <u>checked in for the flight</u> three hours before the departure time.

3 ① counted on ➡ <u>cheated on</u>
② break in ➡ <u>check in</u>

4 ① B: <u>I cheated on the test</u>! Just kidding!
② B: <u>We should check in two hours before the flight</u>.

03 Review

1 ❶ call out ❷ check in ❸ care for ❹ calm down

2 ❶ I'll <u>call him up</u> tomorrow.
❷ Vets <u>care for sick animals</u>.
❸ We have to <u>carry out the mission[carry the mission out]</u>.
❹ Have you ever <u>cheated on an exam</u> before?

3 ❶ I <u>called out</u> very loudly to my sister.
❷ You should <u>care about</u> your health.
❸ <u>Calm down</u> a bit and breathe!
❹ Can I <u>check in</u> at the hotel at 9 a.m.?

4 ❶ A: Did you <u>call</u> him <u>up</u> yesterday?
❷ A: Who <u>cared for</u> the sick animals?

❸ A: When do we <u>check in</u> for the flight?

13 cheer up / chill out

1 ① <u>cheer up</u> the disappointed people
② Sit down and <u>chill out</u>!

2 ① <u>Cheer up and forget about it</u>.
② You look so tense. <u>Just chill out</u>!

3 ① Back up ➡ <u>Cheer up</u>
② Carry out ➡ <u>Chill out</u>

4 ① B: <u>Cheer up, everyone</u>! The game is not over yet.
② A: It was a long day. <u>I need to chill out</u> in front of the TV.

14 catch up with / come across

1 ① <u>catch up with</u> the front-runner
② <u>come across</u> an interesting story

2 ① I can't <u>catch up with him</u>.
② I <u>came across an old school friend</u> in town.

3 ① come up with ➡ <u>catch up with</u>
② came out ➡ <u>came across</u>

4 ① B: <u>I can catch up with her</u> if I run fast.
② A: <u>Have you come across them before</u>?

Answer

15 come out / come over

1 ① come out at last
② come over to my place

2 ① The animals only come out at night.
② Many foreigners came over to Seoul during the Olympics.

3 ① blew out → came out
② gets over → comes over

4 ① A: Your favorite boy band's new album is coming out soon.
② B: Yes, it was lovely. We will come over again soon.

16 come up with / consist of

1 ① come up with a solution
② consist of rice and potatoes

2 ① Never expect him to come up with a brilliant idea.
② Our basketball team consists of nine players.

3 ① caught up with → came up with
② comes mainly of → consists mainly of

4 ① B: Let's ask John. He can always come up with a solution.
② B: Yes, you will. It consists of sandwiches and fruit.

04 Review

1 ① come across ② chill out ③ come over
④ come up with

2 ① Cheer up and forget about it.
② I can't catch up with him.
③ The animals only come out at night.
④ He came up with a solution to our problem.

3 ① Cheer up, everyone!
② I came across an old school friend in town.
③ She sometimes comes over to my house.
④ This book consists of three parts.

4 ① A: I'm so tired. I need to chill out in front of the TV.
② B: I can catch up with her if I run fast.
③ A: My favorite singer's new album is coming out soon.

17 count on / cover up

1 ① count on us
② cover up the mistakes

2 ① You can count on us from now on.
② She tried to cover up the crime.

3 ① get on → count on
② call up → cover up

4 ① A: <u>Can I count on her</u>?

② A: <u>Are you covering up the truth</u> for your friend?

18 cut down on / cut out

1 ① <u>cut down on</u> junk food

② The Internet suddenly <u>cut out</u>.

2 ① I'm trying to <u>cut down on soft drinks</u>.

② Oh my God, <u>the plane's engines have cut out</u>.

3 ① calm down on ➔ <u>cut down on</u>

② put out ➔ <u>cut out</u>

4 ① B: <u>You should cut down on cake</u>!

② A: <u>The radio has cut out</u>.

19 do without / dress up

1 ① <u>do without</u> a smartphone

② <u>dress up</u> like a pirate

2 ① I can't <u>do without your advice</u>!

② She <u>dressed up as a princess</u>.

3 ① do with ➔ <u>do without</u>

② make up ➔ <u>dress up</u>

4 ① B: We ran out. We'll have to <u>do without</u> it today.

② B: I'll go and <u>dress up</u> then.

20 drop by / eat out

1 ① <u>drop by</u> the shop

② <u>eat out</u> every Saturday

2 ① I just <u>dropped by on my way</u> home.

② <u>Let's eat out</u> today.

3 ① pass by ➔ <u>drop by</u>

② eat up ➔ <u>eat out</u>

4 ① A: Can you <u>drop by the shop</u> and get some milk?

② B: <u>Let's eat out tonight</u>.

05 Review

1 ❶ cover up ❷ cut down on ❸ dress up ❹ eat out

2 ❶ You can <u>count on us</u> from now on.

❷ The plane's engines <u>have cut out</u>.

❸ In her work, she cannot <u>do without a computer</u>.

❹ I just <u>dropped by on my way</u> home.

3 ❶ She tried to cover up the truth.

❷ I'm trying to cut down on sweets.

❸ She dressed up as a princess.

❹ Let's eat out today.

4 ❶ B: Sorry. We ran out. We'll have to <u>do without</u> it today.

❷ B: I know. I'm trying to <u>cut down</u> on cake!

Answer

❸ A: Can you drop by the shop and get some milk?

---

21 **fall apart / fall behind**

1 ① My tree house fell apart completely.
② fall behind schedule

2 ① The sandcastle fell apart completely.
② She fell behind with her schoolwork because she missed classes.

3 ① fell down ➜ fell apart
② leave behind ➜ fall behind

4 ① B: Yeah, it looks like it's falling apart.
② B: Yes, I don't want to fall behind.

---

22 **fall off / feel down**

1 ① often fall off the bed
② feel down because of Covid-19

2 ① Please be careful not to fall off the horse.
② I listen to music when I feel down.

3 ① fell behind ➜ fell off
② break down ➜ feel down

4 ① B: He fell off his bicycle while he was riding.
② B: It is okay. I am just feeling down today.

---

23 **figure out / fill out**

1 ① figure out the truth
② fill out the survey

2 ① How did you figure out the meaning of that word?
② Please fill out the form below.

3 ① come out ➜ figure out
② figure out ➜ fill out

4 ① B: I have no idea. I can't figure it out.
② B: Do we need to fill out everything on the sheets?

---

24 **find out / get along with**

1 ① find out the passwords
② get along with classmates

2 ① You will find out the truth soon.
② Luckily, my dog got along with the cats.

3 ① filled out ➜ found out
② get out of ➜ get along with

4 ① A: I finally found out his email address.
② A: My two kids don't seem to get along with each other.

---

06 **Review**

1 ❶ fall apart ❷ fill out ❸ feel down

❹ get along with

2　**❶** She <u>fell behind with</u> her schoolwork.
❷ Please be careful not to <u>fall off the horse</u>.
❸ I cannot <u>figure out the reason</u> behind the error.
❹ I <u>have found out</u> the real name and address.

3　**❶** The sandcastle fell apart completely!
❷ I feel down because of the rain.
❸ Please fill out the landing card now.
❹ I get along with everyone.

4　**❶** B: Yeah, it looks like they're f<u>alling apart</u>.
❷ B: She f<u>ell off</u> her bicycle while she was riding.
❸ B: I have no idea. I can't f<u>igure it out</u>.

25　get around / get away

1　① Word <u>gets around</u>.
② <u>get away</u> from the burning car

2　① She doesn't <u>get around much these days</u>.
② I'm going to <u>get away for a week</u>.

3　① turn around ➔ <u>get around</u>
② get off ➔ <u>get away</u>

4　① B: Good! It was so easy to <u>get around by subway</u>.

② B: I'm going to <u>get away for a week with my family</u>.

26　get back / get into

1　① <u>get back</u> to the topic
② <u>get into</u> hip-hop these days

2　① When did she <u>get back from her trip</u>?
② My dad and I have really <u>gotten into playing boardgames</u>.

3　① take back ➔ <u>get back</u>
② gotten around ➔ <u>gotten into</u>

4　① B: I'll call you when <u>I get back this afternoon</u>.
② A: You're really <u>getting into soccer</u>, aren't you?

27　get off / get on

1　① <u>get off</u> here
② <u>get on</u> the train

2　① We are <u>getting off at the next station</u>.
② I <u>got on the wrong bus</u> this morning.

3　① get on ➔ <u>get off</u>
② put on ➔ <u>get on</u>

4　① A: <u>Where did she get off the bus</u>?
② A: <u>How do you get on a plane</u> if you can't walk?

Answer

28   get out of / get over

1   ① get <u>out</u> <u>of</u> my way
② get <u>over</u> a bad experience

2   ① You have to <u>get out of the flood zone now</u>.
② He <u>can't get over his shyness</u>.

3   ① Get along with ➜ <u>Get out of</u>
② go over ➜ <u>get over</u>

4   ① B: Yes, <u>I want to get out of this small town</u>.
② A: It is hard to <u>get over the death of my dog</u>.

07   Review

1   ❶ <u>get away</u> ❷ <u>get off</u> ❸ <u>get out of</u>
❹ <u>get over</u>

2   ❶ She doesn't <u>get around much</u> these days.
❷ What time will <u>you get back</u>?
❸ Watch your step when you <u>get off the subway</u>.
❹ I hope you <u>get over the flu</u>.

3   ❶ He got around by bike.
❷ I am getting into Latin music these days.
❸ I will get off at the next stop.
❹ Get out of the building! It is falling apart!

4   ① B: Good. It was so easy to <u>get around</u> by subway.
② B: You should <u>get off</u> at this stop.
③ A: I'll <u>get back</u> home this afternoon.

29   get through / get together

1   ① <u>get through</u> the thick forest
② <u>get together</u> for practice

2   ① First, I have to <u>get through the exams</u>.
② Every week they <u>get together to make music</u>.

3   ① get together ➜ <u>get through</u>
② go together ➜ <u>get together</u>

4   ① B: Poor thing! <u>He can't get through the door</u>.
② B: <u>We get together once a month</u>.

30   get up / get well

1   ① <u>get up</u> early in the morning
② will <u>get well</u> with the treatment

2   ① My grandfather never <u>failed to get up early</u>.
② He must <u>help himself to get well</u>.

3   ① get on ➜ <u>get up</u>
② get back ➜ <u>get well</u>

4   ① B: <u>I usually get up at 7:00</u>.
② A: <u>Get well soon</u>. We miss you a lot.

31 give away / give up

1 ① give away her last penny
② give up easily

2 ① I gave away old toys to charity.
② She is never going to give up.

3 ① pass away → give away
② give out → give up

4 ① B: I know but I gave away all of mine last month.
② B: Yes, but I didn't give up.

32 go along with / go by

1 ① go along with his opinion
② Last week went by so fast.

2 ① I'll go along with you this time.
② Time goes by so slowly when you are bored.

3 ① get through with → go along with
② goes over → goes by

4 ① A: I won't go along with her idea on the program.
② B: A sixth grader? Time goes by so quickly.

08 Review

1 ❶ get together ❷ get up ❸ give away ❹ go by

2 ❶ How can we get through the winter?
❷ I hope he will get well soon with the medicine.
❸ She is never going to give up.
❹ Time goes by so slowly when you are bored.

3 ❶ First, I have to get through the doorway.
❷ I get up at 7:30 every day.
❸ We gave away our old clothes to neighbors.
❹ I'll go along with you this time.

4 ❶ B: We get together once a month.
❷ B: I usually get up at 6:00 in the morning.
❸ B: I know, but I'm never going to give up.

33 go off / go over

1 ① go off for a few seconds
② go over a problem

2 ① The alarm goes off at six.
② You should go over your answers to find mistakes.

Answer

3 ① went through ➜ <u>went off</u>
② go by ➜ <u>go over</u>

4 ① B: It's a false alarm. <u>It goes off all the</u>
<u>time</u>.
② A: <u>Go over your homework</u> before you
hand it in.

---

34 go through / grow up

1 ① <u>go through</u> dramatic changes
② <u>grow up</u> like your dad

2 ① He is <u>going through a hard time</u>.
② I <u>grew up in the countryside</u>.

3 ① getting through ➜ <u>going through</u>
② cover up ➜ <u>grow up</u>

4 ① B: Don't worry. We all <u>go through that</u>
<u>stage</u>!
② A: What do you want to be <u>when you</u>
<u>grow up</u>?

---

35 hand down / hand in

1 ① <u>hand down</u> a piece of old furniture
② <u>hand in</u> the evidence to the police

2 ① Jimmy <u>handed down his old shirts</u> to
his younger brother.
② I <u>handed in my homework early this</u>
<u>time</u>.

---

3 ① handed on ➜ <u>handed down</u>
② hand down ➜ <u>hand in</u>

4 ① A: <u>My sister handed down her old</u>
<u>clothes to me</u>.
② B: <u>I handed it in to the police</u>. Is that
okay?

---

36 hang on to / hang out with

1 ① <u>hang on to</u> the rope
② <u>hang out with</u> family

2 ① It is very windy. Please <u>hang on to your</u>
<u>hat tightly</u>.
② I <u>want to hang out with you</u>.

3 ① hang out with ➜ <u>hang on to</u>
② hung up with ➜ <u>hung out with</u>

4 ① B: No, please <u>hang on to your dream</u>!
② B: <u>I hang out with my best friends</u>
every Friday.

---

09 Review

1 ❶ go off ❷ hand in ❸ hang out with
❹ hang on to

2 ❶ Let's <u>go over our schedule</u>.
❷ He <u>is going through</u> a rough patch.
❸ She <u>handed down her old shirts</u>
<u>[handed her old shirts down]</u> to her
younger sister.
❹ I want to <u>hang out with</u> you.

---- 140 ----

3 ① The fire alarm went off for no reason.
② Children grow up so quickly.
③ I handed in the report early this time.
④ Please hang on to the handle.

4 ① B: OMG. The fire alarm went off. Let's go outside.
② A: What do you want to be when you grow up?
③ B: I hang out with my best friend every Friday.

37 hang up / hold back

1 ① Hang up, please.
② hold back a burp

2 ① Don't hang up on me. I need to talk to you.
② Do not hold back the truth.

3 ① hang on ➡ hang up
② call back ➡ hold back

4 ① A: Oh, I have to hang up now. My mom is calling me.
② B: Absolutely. I couldn't hold back my laughter.

38 hold on / hold out

1 ① Please hold on a minute.
② hold out the ticket

2 ① Do you wish to call back or hold on?
② Please hold out your hand.

3 ① hold up ➡ hold on
② held on ➡ held out

4 ① B: Hold on a second. I need a pen and paper.
② A: I've got something for you. Hold out your hand.

39 hold up / hurry up

1 ① hold up the camera
② hurry up with the coffee

2 ① Hold up your hands so I can see what's in them.
② Hurry up or you will be late.

3 ① hold back ➡ hold up
② cheer up ➡ hurry up

4 ① B: Please hold up your hand if you have any questions.
② B: Yes, so hurry up and get dressed!

40 leave for / let (someone) down

1 ① leave for the airport
② Don't let me down.

2 ① Don't forget the camera before you leave for the trip.
② I hope he won't let his fans down.

Answer

3 ① live for → <u>leave for</u>
② letting my parents out → <u>letting my parents down</u>

4 ① B: You didn't know? I'm <u>leaving for France</u>.
② A: I'm sorry for <u>letting you down with the test result</u>.

10 Review

1 ❶ hold out ❷ hang up ❸ hurry up
❹ leave for

2 ❶ Do not <u>hold back the truth[hold the truth back]</u>.
❷ Could you <u>hold on, please</u>?
❸ She will <u>hold up the sign[hold the sign up]</u> for you to see.
❹ I hope he won't <u>let his parents down [let down his parents]</u>.

3 ❶ Please hang up now. I'll call you back.
❷ He held out his arms to me.
❸ We don't have time. We should hurry up.
❹ I am going to leave for America.

4 ❶ B: Absolutely. I couldn't <u>hold back</u> my laughter.
❷ B: <u>Hold on</u> a second. I need a pen and paper.
❸ A: I'm sorry for <u>letting</u> you <u>down</u>.

41 let out / lie down

1 ① <u>let out</u> a scream of pain
② <u>lie down</u> with the dogs

2 ① He <u>let out a cry of disbelief</u>.
② Why don't you <u>lie down and relax</u>?

3 ① went out → <u>let out</u>
② let down → <u>lie down</u>

4 ① B: Yes, she <u>let out a scream</u> when she got hurt.
② B: He went to <u>lie down</u> after the long trip.

42 line up / long for

1 ① <u>Line up</u>, children.
② <u>long for</u> a quieter life

2 ① People should <u>line up to enter the stadium</u>.
② He <u>longed for his dad's advice</u>.

3 ① covered up → <u>lined up</u>
② go for → <u>long for</u>

4 ① B: <u>Line up at the door</u>, children.
② A: I <u>long for a cool breeze</u>!

43 look after / look around

1 ① <u>look after</u> her hamster
② <u>look around</u> the old town

2 ① I'll <u>look after your baby</u> when you're gone.

② What is the best way to <u>look around the city</u>?

3 ① takes after ➔ <u>looks after</u>

② nosing around ➔ <u>looking around</u>

4 ① A: Look at the little girl! <u>She is looking after her baby brother</u>.

② B: We can <u>look around the city</u>. What do you think?

3 ③ The boy <u>looked after homeless cats</u>.

④ A lot of <u>people lined up</u> in a row.

3 ❶ People should line up to enter the stadium.

❷ He let out a deep sigh.

❸ I'll look around my new school.

❹ He's looking for a needle.

4 ❶ B: He is <u>lying down</u> on the sofa.

❷ B: You're right. I <u>long for</u> a cool breeze!

❸ A: Can you <u>look after</u> my hamster until Monday?

---

44 look for / look forward to

1 ① <u>look</u> <u>for</u> the nearest subway station

② <u>look</u> <u>forward</u> <u>to</u> hearing from you

2 ① She's <u>looking for her car key</u>.

② They're <u>looking forward to your visit</u>.

3 ① cared for ➔ <u>looked for</u>

② looking up to ➔ <u>looking forward to</u>

4 ① A: <u>What are you looking for</u>?

② B: <u>I've been looking forward to meeting you, too</u>.

11 Review

1 ❶ long for ❷ look after ❸ let out

❹ look forward to

2 ❶ I'm <u>looking for my earphones</u>.

❷ Why don't <u>you lie down</u> and relax?

45 look into / look up to

1 ① <u>look</u> <u>into</u> the problem

② <u>look</u> <u>up</u> <u>to</u> the legendary director

2 ① The police <u>looked into the cause of the accident</u>.

② They all <u>look up to their teacher</u>.

3 ① look after ➔ <u>look into</u>

② look forward to ➔ <u>look up to</u>

4 ① B: Yes, <u>the police are looking into it</u> in detail.

② B: <u>I look up to my father the most</u>.

46 make out / make up

1 ① <u>make</u> <u>out</u> a person in the photo

② <u>make</u> <u>up</u> an excuse

Answer

2 ① I can't <u>make out the last part of his letter</u>.

② Did you <u>make up the story</u> yourself?

3 ① hold out ➡ <u>make out</u>

② mess up ➡ <u>make up</u>

4 ① B: <u>I can't make them out</u> because they are so tiny.

② B: Honestly, I didn't <u>make up the story</u>!

47 mess up / nose out

1 ① <u>mess up</u> my hair

② <u>nose out</u> his friend's secrets

2 ① The reporter <u>messed up her reputation</u>.

② My dog can <u>nose out his treats anywhere</u>.

3 ① made up ➡ <u>messed up</u>

② picked out ➡ <u>nosed out</u>

4 ① A: Mom, <u>Tommy is messing up my hair</u>!

② A: That reporter always <u>noses out news stories</u>.

48 part with / pass away

1 ① <u>part with</u> her daughter

② <u>pass away</u> soon

2 ① I don't want to <u>part with any of my friends</u>.

② My grandmother <u>passed away last year</u>.

3 ① get into ➡ <u>part with</u>

② passed by ➡ <u>passed away</u>

4 ① B: <u>I can't part with my blanket</u>, Mom! Not yet!

② B: <u>My grandfather passed away</u> when I was young.

12 Review

1 ❶ look up to ❷ look into ❸ pass away ❹ nose out

2 ❶ The reporter <u>messed up her reputation</u> [messed her reputation up].

❷ He <u>made up an excuse</u>[made an excuse up].

❸ She is <u>looking into the accident</u>.

❹ I don't want to <u>part with my best friend</u>.

3 ❶ He looked into the matter.

❷ When did you make up the story?

❸ My dog messed up my room when I went out.

❹ He parted with his children during the war.

4 ❶ B: I <u>look up to</u> my father the most.

❷ B: No. I can't <u>make out</u> the letters because they are so tiny.

❸ B: My grandfather <u>passed away</u> when I was young.

49 pass by / pay off

1 ① pass by the national museum
② pay off in the long run

2 ① I passed by your school today.
② Did your plan pay off in the end?

3 ① passes away ➔ passes by
② put off ➔ pay off

4 ① A: When I go to school, I pass by Central Park.
② B: Yep, but it pays off when I watch movies!

50 pick out / pick up

1 ① pick out fresh vegetables
② pick up Jenny from school

2 ① You can pick two toys out from the list.
② I picked him up from the library.

3 ① picked up ➔ picked out
② packed her up ➔ picked her up

4 ① B: Do you need my help to pick out a dress then?
② B: I'll pick him up from school.

51 point out / pop up

1 ① point out weakness
② pop up at every corner

2 ① I'd like to point out one thing.
② A lot of cafés are popping up now.

3 ① came out ➔ pointed out
② holds up ➔ pops up

4 ① A: Why isn't he pointing out their mistakes?
② B: Yeah, but it pops up sometimes and makes me jump.

52 pull up / put off

1 ① pull up at a gas station
② put off the party

2 ① The taxi pulled up at the entrance.
② Can I put off the meeting?

3 ① put up ➔ pull up
② get off ➔ put off

4 ① A: A suspicious black SUV pulled up behind us.
② A: Don't put off your homework until tomorrow.

13 Review

1 ❶ pop up ❷ pay off ❸ pick up ❹ pick out

2 ❶ I can pick out fresh vegetables.
❷ The delivery man passes by my apartment[passes my apartment by] every day.

Answer

❸ He <u>pointed out the benefits</u> of running.

❹ <u>Please pull up</u> in front of the bus stop.

3
❶ I passed by the bakery today.
❷ Can you help me pick out a gift?
❸ Is it okay to point out errors?
❹ The car pulled up at the entrance.

4
❶ A: When I go to the library, I <u>pass by</u> Central Park.
❷ B: My mom will <u>pick</u> me <u>up</u> from school.
❸ A: Don't p<u>ut off</u> today's work until tomorrow.

53 put on / put out

1
① <u>put on</u> a helmet
② <u>put out</u> the blaze

2
① I <u>put on my clothes</u> in a hurry.
② Dad ran into the kitchen to <u>put out the fire</u>.

3
① put it out ➜ <u>put it on</u>
② go out ➜ <u>put out</u>

4
① B: Before you go out, <u>you should put on a jacket</u>.
② A: <u>The firefighters are putting out the fire</u>.

54 put up / put up with

1
① <u>put up</u> a notice
② <u>put up with</u> his rude behavior

2
① I <u>put up my umbrella</u>.
② The teacher doesn't <u>put up with students' lateness</u>.

3
① put out ➜ <u>put up</u>
② hang out with ➜ <u>put up with</u>

4
① A: <u>Can you put up the curtains for me</u>?
② B: <u>How do you put up with that</u>?

55 rely on / rule out

1
① <u>rely on</u> natural gas
② <u>rule out</u> the bad options

2
① We should <u>rely on green energy</u> in the future.
② We can't <u>rule out the existence of other life</u> in the universe.

3
① put on ➜ <u>rely on</u>
② points him out ➜ <u>rules him out</u>

4
① B: Indeed, as children we <u>rely on our parents</u> for everything.
② A: <u>The solution was ruled out</u> because it was too expensive.

56 run after / run away

1
① run after the bus
② run away from home

2
① A policeman was running after a thief from 100 meters behind.
② He just wanted to run away and hide.

3
① looked after ➡ ran after
② take away ➡ run away

4
① B: Some dogs are running after a fox.
② B: He saw a wild bear and ran away.

14 Review

1
❶ put up with ❷ run away ❸ put out
❹ rule out

2
❶ I put up the flag[put the flag up].
❷ You should put on a jacket[put a jacket on].
❸ A boy is running after the bus.
❹ Many people rely on the Internet for getting information.

3
❶ I put my hat on in a hurry.
❷ He put up a flag in front of his school.
❸ We should rely on green energy in the future.
❹ A dog is running after a rabbit.

4
❶ A: The firefighters are putting out the fire.
❷ B: How do you put up with that?

❸ B: He saw you and ran away.

57 run down / run for

1
① My watch has run down.
② run for President

2
① If a machine runs down, people cannot use the machine.
② You should run for mayor.

3
① calm down ➡ run down
② long for ➡ run for

4
① B: The battery has run down but there's no power outlet.
② A: Senator King will run for re-election next year.

58 run into / run out of

1
① run into serious difficulties
② run out of milk

2
① She ran into Chris at the bus terminal.
② They have run out of ideas.

3
① looked into ➡ ran into
② gotten out of ➡ run out of

4
① B: I ran into Jenny while I was walking on Apple Street.
② B: Nothing. It just ran out of gas.

Answer

59 see off / send for

1 ① <u>see off</u> soldiers to the front line
② <u>sent for</u> a doctor immediately

2 ① Thank you for <u>coming all the way to see me off</u>.
② Please <u>send for a police officer</u> right away.

3 ① picked me up ➜ <u>saw me off</u>
② sent her assistant with ➜ <u>sent her assistant for</u>

4 ① B: I'm <u>seeing off my brother</u> at the train station.
② B: Quick, <u>send for an ambulance</u>!

60 set out / set up

1 ① <u>set out</u> to buy food
② <u>set up</u> the equipment

2 ① They <u>set out on their trip</u> this morning.
② She <u>set up the tent by herself</u>.

3 ① took out ➜ <u>set out</u>
② took up ➜ <u>set up</u>

4 ① A: Fantastic! The rain stopped <u>before we set out</u>!
② B: My dad <u>set up the telescope</u> for me last month.

15 Review

1 ❶ set out ❷ run for ❸ run into
❹ run out of

2 ❶ He <u>set out on</u> his trip yesterday.
❷ They have <u>run out of</u> ideas.
❸ Thank you for coming all the way to <u>see me off</u>.
❹ If <u>a machine runs down</u>, people cannot use the machine.

3 ❶ The battery has run down.
❷ We are going to run out of gas.
❸ My parents saw me off at the airport.
❹ My brother set up the computer for me.

4 ❶ B: The battery has r<u>un down</u>.
❷ B: I r<u>an into</u> him when I went by Sunrise Park.
❸ B: Please, s<u>end for</u> an ambulance!

61 settle into / show off

1 ① <u>settle into</u> a new house
② <u>show off</u> her abilities

2 ① They need time to <u>settle into the big city</u>.
② Some people take pictures to <u>show off their products</u>.

3 ① get into ➜ <u>settle into</u>
② getting off ➜ <u>showing off</u>

4 ① A: How are your kids settling into their new school?

② B: He wanted to show off his new smart watch.

62 show up / sleep in

1 ① show up on the screen

② sleep in every weekend

2 ① He showed up an hour later.

② Jacob slept in again, so he was late for school.

3 ① hanged up → showed up

② check in → sleep in

4 ① B: Yes, but I'll be surprised if they show up on time.

② B: Not much. I slept in until 11:00 a.m.

63 stand for / stand out

1 ① The letters 'U.N.' stand for 'United Nations.'

② stand out among people

2 ① VIP' stands for 'Very Important Person.'

② Paul's performance really stands out.

3 ① care for → stand for

② cut out → stood out

4 ① A: What does 'KFC' stand for?

② B: Yes, she stands out among people.

64 stand up for / stay up late

1 ① stand up for your rights

② used to stay up late

2 ① He stood up for everyone on his team.

② Did you stay up late last night?

3 ① stand for → stand up for

② put up with → stay up late

4 ① B: She always stands up for us.

② B: I stayed up very late last night.

16 Review

1 ❶ settle into ❷ stand out ❸ sleep in ❹ stand up for

2 ❶ Jacob slept in again, so he was late for school.

❷ They started showing off their language skills.

❸ 'VIP' stands for 'Very Important Person.'

❹ She always stands up for us.

3 ❶ He wants to show off a new hat.

❷ He finally showed up on the stage.

❸ 'DIY' stands for 'Do It Yourself.'

❹ Did you stay up late last night?

4 ❶ A: How are your pets settling into the new house?

❷ B: Not much. I slept in until 12:00.

❸ B: Yes, she stands out among people.

Answer

65 stretch out / switch off

1 ① <u>stretch out</u> his long legs
② Would you just <u>switch off</u>?

2 ① <u>Stretch out your arms</u> and breathe in
fresh air.
② I <u>switch off when</u> he starts talking
about cars.

3 ① pointed out → <u>stretched out</u>
② see off → <u>switch off</u>

4 ① A: Could you move your seat forward?
<u>I can't stretch out my legs</u>.
② B: Not really. <u>The students switch off</u>
as soon as he starts speaking.

66 take after / take apart

1 ① <u>take after</u> my aunt
② <u>take apart</u> a TV

2 ① The girl <u>takes after her grandmother</u>.
② I <u>took apart the computer</u> to fix it.

3 ① ask after → <u>take after</u>
② Taking away → <u>Taking apart</u>

4 ① B: No, <u>she takes after her father</u>.
② B: It's broken, so <u>I took it apart</u>.

67 take away / take back

1 ① <u>take away</u> the stress
② <u>take back</u> what I said

2 ① Please <u>take away the dirty dishes</u>.
② I am sorry. I <u>take back my words</u>.

3 ① run away → <u>take away</u>
② call back → <u>take back</u>

4 ① B: Because <u>she took away all their cell
phones</u>.
② A: I think <u>you should take back what
you said</u> about Don!

68 take off / take out

1 ① The planes are waiting to <u>take off</u>.
② <u>take out</u> some money from her wallet

2 ① Three planes are <u>taking off at the same
time</u>.
② You may need to have a tooth <u>taken
out today</u>.

3 ① getting off → <u>taking off</u>
② found out → <u>took out</u>

4 ① B: Sorry, you can't. The plane will <u>take
off in about 2 minutes</u>.
② A: <u>Could you take out the suitcase</u>
from the overhead bin?

Review

1 ❶ stretch out ❷ take off ❸ take apart
❹ take back

2 ❶ I am sorry. I take back my words[take my words back].
❷ People say I take after my uncle.
❸ If you don't care about sports, switch off now.
❹ He took out some chocolate[took some chocolate out] from the box.

3 ❶ Would you just switch off, please?
❷ Susan takes after her mother.
❸ Please take away the dirty dishes.
❹ He took a book out from the bookshelf.

4 ❶ B: Stretch out your arms and count to 10.
❷ B: It's not working, so I took it apart.
❸ A: Oh, I can't take out the suitcase from the overhead bin.

69 **take over / take up**

1 ① take over her duties
② take up too much room

2 ① I will take over Amy's job for a week.
② It won't take up much of your time.

3 ① got over ➜ took over
② hold up ➜ take up

4 ① B: I took over the job from Jarvis last month.
② B: Sorry, the team meeting took up most of my morning.

70 **tell apart / think over**

1 ① tell different Asian races apart
② think over her words

2 ① They look alike, so I can't tell them apart.
② Please think over your position very carefully.

3 ① take apart ➜ tell apart
② get over ➜ think over

4 ① B: Yes, I can't tell them apart.
② A: Think over the offer very carefully before you answer.

71 **throw away / throw up**

1 ① throw away the leftovers
② go to the toilet and throw up

2 ① You should throw it away in the garbage bin.
② I feel like I am going to throw up.

3 ① get away ➜ throw away
② grow up ➜ throw up

Answer

4 ① A: I don't want to <u>throw away this old chair</u>.

② B: I feel sick. <u>I'm going to throw up</u> in the toilet.

72 tie up / try on

1 ① <u>tie up</u> the balloon
② <u>try on</u> the brown coat

2 ① She <u>ties up her hair</u> every morning.
② Let me <u>try on the red blouse</u>.

3 ① line up ➜ <u>tie up</u>
② put several outfits up ➜ <u>tried several outfits on</u>

4 ① A: <u>Should I tie up the present</u> before we give it to Dad?
② B: <u>Can I try on the jacket</u>?

18 Review

1 ❶ throw away ❷ take up ❸ try on
❹ think over

2 ❶ Can you <u>tell the dogs apart[tell apart the dogs]</u> from one another?
❷ He <u>took over the business[took the business over]</u> from his grandfather.
❸ She <u>ties up her hair[ties her hair up]</u> every morning.
❹ I feel like I'm going <u>to throw up</u>.

3 ❶ I will take over the work for a week.
❷ The twins look alike, so I can't tell them apart.
❸ I think I am going to throw up.
❹ Tie up your shoelaces, or you will fall.

4 ❶ A: Can you <u>t</u>ell the two flags <u>apart</u>?
❷ A: Should I <u>t</u>hrow away these old books?
❸ A: Can I <u>t</u>ry on these jeans?

73 try out / turn around

1 ① <u>try out</u> a new skateboard
② <u>turn around</u> to see me

2 ① Would you like to <u>try out an electric car</u>?
② He <u>turned around and ran away</u>.

3 ① set out ➜ <u>tried out</u>
② Get around ➜ <u>Turn around</u>

4 ① B: <u>I'm trying out my new running shoes</u> before the game.
② B: <u>Turn around</u> and you'll find it.

74 turn down / turn into

1 ① <u>turn down</u> a job offer
② <u>turn into</u> a good student

2 ① Why did you <u>turn down Emma's invitation</u>?

② Do you know <u>how milk turns into cheese</u>?

5 ① handed down → <u>turned down</u>
② look into → <u>turn into</u>

4 ① B: That's a steal! <u>How can I turn that down</u>?
② B: Because his new robot <u>can turn into a car</u>.

---

75 **turn off / turn on**

1 ① <u>turn off</u> the light
② <u>turn on</u> the air conditioner

2 ① I <u>turn off the alarm clock</u> after I get up.
② Can you tell me how to <u>turn on this cell phone</u>?

5 ① put off → <u>turn off</u>
② Try on → <u>Turn on</u>

4 ① A: Is it okay to <u>turn off the computer now</u>?
② B: You need to <u>turn on the light</u>.

---

76 **turn out / turn over**

1 ① <u>turn out</u> to be groundless
② The crabs <u>turn over</u> by themselves.

2 ① I'm glad that things <u>turned out well</u> in the end.

② The truck <u>turned over and injured</u> the driver.

5 ① took out → <u>turned out</u>
② took over → <u>turned over</u>

4 ① B: Don't worry. <u>Everything will turn out okay</u>.
② A: The doctor will <u>ask you to turn over</u> onto your back.

---

19 **Review**

1 ❶ turn down ❷ try out ❸ turn off
❹ turn over

2 ❶ <u>He turned around</u> and ran away.
❷ I'm bored. <u>Turn on the music[Turn the music on]</u>, please.
❸ Why did <u>you turn down</u> her invitation?
❹ I'm glad that things <u>turned out well</u> in the end.

5 ❶ Please turn around at the end of the road.
❷ The rumor turned out to be true.
❸ It's too cold. Can you turn on the heater?
❹ How does a caterpillar turn into a butterfly?

4 ❶ A: Would you like to <u>try out</u> this new phone?
❷ B: That's a steal. How can I <u>turn that down</u>?

Answer

❸ A: Don't forget to <u>turn off</u> the computer before you leave.

77 turn to / wait on

1 ① <u>turn to</u> games and the Internet
② <u>wait on</u> two customers at once

2 ① I always <u>turn to books when I am in trouble</u>.
② I am going to <u>wait on them</u> today.

3 ① look to ➔ <u>turn to</u>
② rely on ➔ <u>wait on</u>

4 ① B: No, <u>you are the only person I can turn to</u>.
② B: <u>I'm too tired to wait on you</u>. Get it yourself!

78 watch out (for) / wear out

1 ① <u>Watch out</u>, everyone!
② brakes <u>wear</u> <u>out</u>

2 ① You will fall into the pool <u>if you don't watch out</u>!
② Why do my shoes <u>wear out faster</u> on one side?

3 ① put out ➔ <u>watch out</u>
② picked out ➔ <u>wore out</u>

4 ① B: We were told to <u>watch out for fake jewelry</u>.

② B: <u>They didn't wear out quickly</u>.

79 work out / wrap up

1 ① <u>work out</u> in the evening
② <u>wrap up</u> the project

2 ① I <u>work out three times a week</u>.
② It's time to <u>wrap up what you are doing</u>.

3 ① Standing out ➔ <u>Working out</u>
② take up ➔ <u>wrap up</u>

4 ① B: <u>I work out every day</u>.
② B: I will <u>have wrapped things up</u> by noon. So, shortly after that.

80 write down / zoom in

1 ① <u>write down</u> important points
② <u>zoom in</u> on the background

2 ① I'll <u>write down the phone number</u> for her.
② She <u>zoomed in on the subway station</u> on the map.

3 ① turn that down ➔ <u>write that down</u>
② settle in ➔ <u>zoom in</u>

4 ① A: <u>Writing things down</u> helps me to remember them better.
② B: <u>By zooming in on the picture</u> you can see the person's face better.

1 ❶ wait on ❷ wear out ❸ zoom in
❹ wrap up

2 ❶ You will fall into the pool if you <u>don't watch out</u>!

❷ <u>I work out</u> three times a week.

❸ Who does <u>he turn to</u> when he feels sad?

❹ I'll <u>write down the important points [write the important points down]</u>.

3 ❶ I turn to my older sister.

❷ Hey, watch out! There are rocks on the road.

❸ Working out every day is good for your health.

❹ I can't see it. Can you zoom in on his face?

4 ❶ A: Oh, no! Look at the rug. It's w<u>orn out</u>.

❷ A: It's time to w<u>rap up</u> what you are doing.

❸ B: W<u>riting</u> things <u>down</u> helps me remember them better.